FRANK FONTANA'S
*DIRTY LITTLE SECRETS OF DESIGN

FRANK FONTANA'S
*DIRTY LITTLE SECRETS OF DESIGN

PHOTOGRAPHS BY BRIAN WILLETTE

Stewart, Tabori & Chang, New York

CONTENTS

Introduction: Frank's Way

A Realistic, Thoughtful Approach to Stylish DIY Home Design   7

PART One: The Blueprint

The Foundation of High-Style, Low-Cost Decorating   17

Chapter One: High-Style, Low-Cost Principles of Planning

Frank's Plan for Creating Beauty on a Budget   19

Chapter Two: Know Your Design Style

Learn the Language of Design to Help You Save a Dime   27

Chapter Three: Walls of Wonder

Using Color, Texture, and More to Create the Best Environment for Your Design   45

Chapter Four: Going Green for Less

A List of Green Options Without Those that Wallop Your Wallet   67

PART Two: Transforming Your Home

A Room-by-Room Guide to Infusing Your Home with Style   79

Chapter Five: Entryways

Making a Perfect First Impression   81

Chapter Six: Living Spaces

Designing the Heart of Your Home   97

Chapter Seven : Sleeping Spaces

Designing the Perfect Restful Nest   115

Chapter Eight: Kitchens

Whip Up a High-Style Tasty Space   133

Chapter Nine: Office Spaces

Your Sanctuary for Success   153

Chapter Ten: Entertaining Spaces

Spaces for Parties, Dining, and Media Centers   169

Chapter Eleven: Outdoor Spaces

Add a Room to Your Home—No Walls Needed   187

Resources   199

DIY Index   201

Special Thanks   203

INTRODUCTION
FRANK'S WAY

A realistic, thoughtful approach to stylish DIY home design

Interior decorating and home styling can be very difficult to teach. Achieving true style on a budget—even harder. Let's face it; if it were easy to master, then I would be out of a job. Well, I suppose I could hit up some of my buddies from the old 'hood for work on a construction site (I do, after all, know my way around a drill and pneumatic nail gun). Construction sure isn't my first choice, though I'll play the tough-guy card when I have to; it's hands-on home design and (that's right, I'll say it!) decorating that really captures me. The job I have is an important and creative one that I love. In light of periodic economic nose dives, my employment is not something I take for granted. I've always made it a policy not to take my clients, or their budgets, for granted either.

People hire me to save them time and money. I know what you're thinking: Hiring an interior decorator ranks just below having a full-time chauffeur in the list of habits reserved for the rich. Now you have this book, though, so that's not the case anymore. I'll guide you through every aspect of the process I go through on behalf of every one of my clients, as well as each of the guests on my hit television show, HGTV's *Design on a Dime*. Though I'm not there in person to do the building, shopping, planning, and furnishing for you, that doesn't mean you can't take my advice and turn your space into the nest or palace or anything in between that you'll love to live in. Along the way, I'll drop some knowledge that will save you some major scratch—and plenty of headaches to boot.

Maybe you need help with one project—a single room that has been lying cluttered or ugly for too long and needs rehabilitation *now*. I humbly submit that after employing some of my tips and Dirty Little Secrets to keeping costs lower than low, you might just venture into a new project—maybe upgrade another space with the money you saved. Not only will you find cheap solutions for staples of any well-designed room, but I'll show you ways to bring in lots of unique style with uncanny, affordable, and almost effortless tweaks—tweaks I learned by doing room makeovers on a very tight budget. Also, to shine some tasteful lamplight on the obvious, saving money is not just for when times are tough.

So my goal is to impart my best budget-conscious advice on designing anyplace into *your space*. How, exactly, are we going to accomplish this?

I'll show you how to take Everything in a room and, using my principles of design, rearrange it so that a few introductions will create a huge influx of style and cohesion.

What do I mean by *Everything* with a capital *E*? I mean not just the rug, the lamps, the curtains, and the seats. Not just the wall hangings, the plants, the windows, and the drawers. Each room is composed of so much more. Each room has a distinctive feel. It's something that hits people within their first thirty seconds in a space, and they know whether they like it or not. (That same intuition guides us through the pitfalls of blind dating . . . ideally.) That *thing* (call it an aura, a vibe, a resonance, an aesthetic . . . whatever suits you) is what we are trying to craft when we design a room. Tuning the feel is central to my design method. It is the basis of what I address with my **Quantum Design Element** (*Q.D.E.*).

That's right, we're dabbling in quantum mechanics. Don't worry, though—protective eyewear is only

ONE OF MY FAVORITE VIGNETTES IN MY LOFT. BEYOND THE WINDOW IS A GREAT VIEW OF CHICAGO *

mandatory when you're working with power tools. It is the quantum nature of things that dictates how they interact with one another in palpable ways. The specific things we're concerned about in this case are the contents of your room, including the empty space. I want to suggest that this space isn't actually empty. It's already quite full of feeling.

Whether you rented or bought, you paid for the space that you are about to transform. There were probably even some things you liked about it. Personally, when I bought my loft in Chicago, I loved the exposed brick, the high ceilings, and the worn wood. But it wasn't really those individual things that grabbed me. It was the way they existed in the space. The feeling they exuded told a story—an almost audible one of how this place, my new home, had been carved out of its urban surroundings. I listened to the voice of the space while I decorated it, choosing stressed leather instead of sleek new stuff and breaking out the sandpaper to wear down some of the wood accents on the furniture I built and bought.

There are so many ways to change the look of things you already have or that you buy (like when I sandpapered some of the accents in my home). I have a whole slew of what I call my *Look for Less* principles. These are methods that will allow you to look at even the most finely tuned, expensive design and duplicate it in your own home for a fraction of the price. All that's required is ingenuity and initiative. I've spent a whole career decorating on tight budgets, building up ingenious ideas for achieving certain looks for less, and I've provided tips and instructions throughout the book. All you need is to take the initiative and apply them to the look you're going for. Sometimes the beautiful spaces in design magazines feel out of reach—but not this time!

Many of the pictures in this book are from gorgeous homes that seem unattainable. My Look for Less principles, though, will take cues from these homes and explain how with less money, a touch of elbow grease, and ingenuity you can achieve the same effects in your space.

It will help to have an idea of what result you're trying to reach. My Q.D.E. is a method that encourages you to pay attention to the feeling you're building in your space. Pay attention to each piece you bring to a room and how the new feeling resonates with everything already present. What does this mean for us? It means we are not simply going to take what manufacturers provide us with and just plop it into a nice spot. (That's not to say I won't provide ample plopping advice.) We are going to pay attention to not just where we plop but what adjustments we might make to objects so they resonate more beautifully.

It's like making a sandwich.

It's a generally recognized as a fact of the universe: A bad sandwich can come from the same ingredients that make up a perfect sandwich. It's all about how they are put together. If you use vinaigrette you can't just drizzle it anywhere—it needs to soak into the bread. And if you go overboard with the vinaigrette you're in trouble . . . you need to start over or at least get a new piece of bread. (Fortunately home design, unlike sandwich artistry, is more forgiving of trial and error.)

It's also like putting together an outfit.

Everybody knows an outfit is more than the sum of its parts. If you have a gorgeous pearl necklace you're not going to wear it with sweatpants. But anyone who knows fashion also knows that you don't need to spend as much on the pants as you did on the necklace for the two items to complement each other and make each other look better than when alone. You also know that your favorite outfit has more value for you when you can remember the story of how you got every piece: maybe the necklace is your grandmother's and the pants were bought from your friends' upstart boutique. These stories let you enjoy that outfit more than if you just bought it all at a department store. The same is true for home design.

With a sandwich, once you find that perfect combination for your favorite, it's something you'll be able to go to whenever you want some good, comfortable deliciousness. The same is true for your space—once you find the combination you like, it will nourish you as constantly and as comfortably as your favorite food.

With an outfit, you might let it continuously evolve while keeping a few key items. These are most likely to be those that have personal significance to you. They give you a positive feeling when you see them, even just in the closet. That positive energy can come from décor in a room, too.

In my experience, she who has mastered her personal fashion truly understands herself. She who has mastered sandwich making truly understands the universe. Mastering home design is as important as either (okay, maybe a little less important than a perfect sandwich). No matter which is *most* important to you, the truth is that home design borrows from both because it combines the need to satisfy your own taste, the taste of others, and the harmony of every item you put together.

It's tempting, when decorating a room, to approach it more like a photographer than a chef or fashion designer—or even more romantically, like a painter. Negative and positive space. Presence and absence. There's a catch though: You're present, not absent! A room is more like food and fashion than a picture because you don't just look at it, you live with it and in it. You had better be sure you love it!

So, one of the most important user tips for my Q.D.E. is to go with your taste and let that tell you what works together. Also, pay attention to the story behind things when you're wondering what should stay and what should go.

At this point you might be feeling a little nervous. You may or may not have a degree in quantum physics, and even if you do, you're doing this in your free time away from the laboratory. Gotta separate work from play, right? So before you grow too concerned about messing with the time-space continuum, let me lay out the rest of the practical tenets of Q.D.E.

I have unified three basic design principles that the Q.D.E. can be universally applied to, no matter what the style of design: it's all about *function, ambiance,* and *cohesion*. I can promise you that following these three principles will, before you know it, allow you to complete the most essential step in home design . . . the design!

1. FUNCTION

It's common to say a room needs "a sense of purpose." A *sense?* Does a fashion designer have a *sense* of how to make a dress? No! She knows the process down to the stitch. Your room needs a very clear, very functional purpose. What will you use it for? Is this space used primarily for cooking, sitting, entertaining, welcoming, storing, practicing handstands, or what? Your décor should be easy to use and made to suit your lifestyle. The only stuff it's okay to leave in a place where it's not effortlessly ready for use is stuff that plays a role in the room's secondary, or special occasion, function. (Extra chairs for entertaining more guests than normal, for example, can be stashed out of the way.) Apply the Q.D.E. principle by envisioning the largest pieces—the ones that by their very size contribute lots to the room's feel—as serving the room's central purpose. An object meant for pure decoration that is going to take up most of the floor space doesn't align with the Q.D.E. Forgetting functionality is like wearing a beautiful new cardigan in July or throwing aged prosciutto on a sandwich when what you are craving is turkey.

2. AMBIANCE

This is where you can really flex the creative potential of the Q.D.E. Ambiance, the general feeling of an environment, is aided by the "double Us": unity and uniqueness. Create spaces that elicit a distinct feel—a furniture theme or color scheme—is a great method, but there are more. (I'll show you how much more in the coming chapters.) The unchangeable elements of the space (shape, architectural elements, windows, and entryways) are where you should start building your ambiance. Again, try to listen to what story the room tells on its own and build from there (the most basic things like location—the middle of a city or a forest—can clue you in to the story). Next you need to identify aspects of objects that enhance that story, like the stressed leather of the chairs in my apartment. Once you identify unifying components of the objects you're decorating with, use the Q.D.E. to distribute them. Think of this like adding seasoning to your sandwich: Taste the result after each adjustment. It's also like tailoring clothes to find the perfect fit, except you can do it yourself. Fortunately, rearranging things in a room and getting it wrong is less disastrous, and more reversible, than hemming your pants too short or putting too much salt and pepper on your turkey club. (I know, I know: You can scrape it off, but you never really get it all, do you?)

3. COHESION

This is the final act of pulling it all together. After coming up with a room's worth of ideas in your head or sketching them out, perform a quick inventory. Will everything function as a whole, even when individual pieces are laid next to each other? If you have several different types of ambient presence, are they adding to each other instead of clashing? Are there any areas of the room that are neglected? In this final test, I want you to imagine what the empty space will feel like in your new room. But the ultimate test of cohesion, whether your design as you now envision it will work, is the sandwich test. Is it something you will get excited to come back to every day? A good combination of healthy and tasty? If so, you passed the certification test for using the Quantum Design Element.

If you've taken the time to apply the Q.D.E. to your thoughts about your project, you now have a vision. I hope it's more specific than when you cracked this book for the first time. If not, never fear. Keep the Q.D.E. and its three components in mind and move on. Your vision can be fuzzy at this point, and probably should be. In Chapter One we'll fit everything to a specific plan.

Now that we've talked a little about the underpinnings of my design method, we'll move on to more specific advice. Lots of it. You didn't think I was going to tell you

FRANK FONTANA'S *Dirty Little* SECRETS OF DESIGN

to look at your room as if it were some sort of sandwich and then just say "go get 'em, tiger," did you? No way: I'm going to offer you original projects, fun new approaches to details, shortcuts that don't show, and loads more Dirty Little Secrets to bring more to your project for less.

And just because my ultimate dirty little secret, my Quantum Design Element, isn't so dirty after all, doesn't mean you should go spilling the beans about it. So what if it came out of a physics laboratory? If some of those guys from the old neighborhood found out I was a closet nerd, they might shake me down for almost twenty years of milk money! And you don't want that to happen, because with all that small change we can make some snazzy throw pillows.

INEXPENSIVE MATERIALS

For every gorgeous, luxurious, cost-prohibitive material in existence there is an inexpensive alternative if you just apply some effort and ingenuity. Here is a list of my favorite money-saving materials and what they can replace:

* *Medium Density Fiberboard (MDF):* Replace any wood in a project with MDF. This material is incredibly cheap because it is essentially compressed sawdust and glue. It is durable and easy to cut. One problem is that there is no grain to it, so finishing and/or wood graining is a must.

* *Coffee and tea:* Replace dark wood stains with a mixture that is three parts strongly brewed coffee with four or five black tea bags in it and one part water. Make sure this stain has steeped for about a day before using it.

* *Green building materials:* Most green building products are either cheaper to use than normal material or offer savings incentives from agencies interested in promoting sustainable building. See my *Great Green List* ("Going Green for Less," page 67) for an extensive catalog of eco-friendly materials.

* *Wood for building:* When buying lumber for building projects, you'll usually need either 1x4s ("one-by-fours") or 2x4s ("two-by-fours"). These are very common dimensions for lumber, and anyone selling wood to you will know what you are asking for immediately. That said, if you are salvaging and wondering about what to look for, you'll need to know a few things: The first number refers to the depth of the wood and the second number refers to the width; the length varies depending on your project. Also, in reality the dimensions aren't even one inch by four inches and two inches by four inches! A one-by-four is really ¾ inches deep and 3 ½ inches wide. A two-by-four is really 1 ½ inches deep and 3 ½ inches wide. Plywood and MDF typically come in sheets of four feet by eight feet and vary in thickness, typically from 1 ¼ inches all the way up to 1 ¾ inches.

You should also be aware of the different qualities of building woods as this will greatly affect your price and potentially your project. They are:

Utility-grade/Framing lumber: This grade is good but has some irregularities and deformities such as knots, pitch lines, and some rough edges. Often, framing lumber is used in areas where the wood won't be exposed. **Stud-grade lumber**: Better quality than utility/framing lumber but you'll need to be selective when buying it to find good, straight studs for your walls. *Premium-grade lumber*: This is the best quality wood; you really only need it in instances where the wood is left exposed and has to have fewer flaws simply for the sake of good looks.

FRANK'S FAVE FAUX FINISHES

I have a saying: If you can't afford it, faux it! Faux finishes are an essential way to raise the style of both refurbished and new pieces of furniture while keeping costs lower than you've ever thought possible. You can make inexpensive, generic materials look like rare luxury fare with a little effort and *very* little cash spent. Throughout the book I'll provide tips on when to use which faux finishes. Here is a rundown of what you'll need for each look and how to apply it.

COLOR WASH

The Feeling: Depending on the glaze, color, and surface used, the look can vary, but I love using a sun-kissed yellow and burnt sienna to create a rich Tuscan interior, or timeworn leather material by layering more brown tones.

Materials: paint sponge (or rag), primer, main color paint, color glaze, paint brushes, painter's tape

How to: Color washing allows for plenty of freedom of technique. Simply tape off the area you want to apply the wash to, prime it, and paint a coat of your base layer. The special part comes when you dip a damp sponge or soft rag in the colored glaze and apply it to the already painted surface after it dries. Be creative and unsystematic with how you apply the glaze, and you'll end with a unique piece of handiwork every time! Just make sure the rag or sponge isn't dripping with paint when you dab. It's better to start light and build up with layering.

DRYBRUSH

The Feeling: Drybrushing is a painting technique that adds a distressed or worn look to any item. While you may think this fits best in a country setting, it also blends well in an urban environment, simulating the sort of rawness that makes things like exposed brick walls and timber beams so popular in city apartments. It's that little touch of detail that can authenticate a distinctive, aged look. Envision that imperfect bit of whitewash, rust, or burnishing that tells the story of an object's existence. Drybrushing is a big asset when going for a Shabby Chic look. No primer is needed, because the color paint plays that part.

Materials: color paint, white paint, paint brushes

How to: Drybrushing is all about incomplete layers. Use the color paint as a base coat for your item and let that dry. Then, put only a small amount of white paint on the brush and drag the brush in a long band across the surface so the white does not consistently cover the area you brushed. Layering is key here, so start light and use successive layers of dryly brushed white paint to slowly fill the look in without fully covering the base color.

WHITEWASHING

The Feeling: This adds a pleasant country element to any wood surface. The color of the material will show through the whitewash, which is thinner than normal paint.

Materials: white primer, water, paint brushes

How to: Use a homemade mix: half white primer and half water. Stir it well. Paint this over natural materials or another dried coat of colored paint. The water thins out the primer just enough to allow a transparency similar to drybrushing, but it is spread more evenly.

TEXTURING

The Feeling: This can range from a time-worn mood filled with Old-

FRANK FONTANA'S DIRTY LITTLE SECRETS OF DESIGN

World charm and eloquence to a geometric and modern look, depending on the pattern and tools you use to apply it. More subdued texturing has a modern feel, which can also be added to by using bold colors instead of traditional earth tones.

Materials: trowel, plaster, tint(s); glaze and paint are optional afterward

How to: Texturing with plaster is far easier than people think. Either add tints to your wet plaster and mix them in or leave it without tint. To create a Spanish style, a popular Old-World look, start simple by scooping some plaster with the trowel and spreading it in a repeating rainbow pattern across the surface. You could also move directly into plaster masterwork by spreading the plaster more irregularly. After the first coat dries, adding a second (and even third) layer with a different tint can enhance the effect. Even out each layer with the trowel to keep it flat and modern.

METALLICS

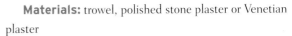

The Feeling: Metallic finishes can be luxurious and even opulent, rusticated, or ultra-modern depending on color and sheen. They are especially eye catching as accents on walls.

Materials: metallic paint, latex primer, paint brushes, painter's tape

How to: The number of metals you can mimic is almost infinite because of the variety of products out there—and most of them are premixed, which makes them even easier to find. Silver and gold are just the beginning. Seek out rust-activating paints if you want an antique or patina metallic look. Another wonderful metallic finish is shimmer stone by Modern Masters, a metal-based plaster that you apply using the same method as with texturing.

POLISHED STONE

The Feeling: Polished stone is a classic look that has been a favorite for ages. Now it is available without heavy lifting or draining your wallet.

Materials: trowel, polished stone plaster or Venetian plaster

How to: Using the trowel, spread the plaster in an even, flat layer over the surface. This is an easy three-coat process if you take care to even out each coat as you go. Pay attention to which way the trowel marks go, because with many products you can manipulate the mineral coloration of the finished product with the trowel. When dry, burnish the plaster to create a marblelike luster.

WOOD GRAINING

The Feeling: Rich, handcrafted, and organic. Because there is no limit to the woods you can mimic (or make up by using experimental colorations!), wood graining can make cheap, grainless MDF look like the rarest prized hardwoods: think mahogany, cherry, and zebra wood.

Materials: MDF or other inexpensive wood product, latex paint, glaze, wood-graining rocker, paint brushes

How to: We'll use the example of an oak wood effect. Brush on your first layer of latex paint in a tan color. When that dries, brush on a few strips of a dark brown glaze and use the wood-graining rocker on the glaze while it is still wet. Continue painting and rocking strips of glaze until the surface is covered. Be amazed at the results and be sure to experiment with new colors and graining patterns for the rocker. Wood-graining rockers are available at most paint stores. The rocker will probably become your new best friend.

STENCILING

The Feeling: Work smarter, not harder! Art is in the head, not in the hand. A stencil can be a pattern or an individual art piece. Bring some accomplished artistry to your space by adding a stencil or a series of them; there is no limit to the interest you can add by using stencils—they are a staple in my toolbox. But don't overdo it, or your place could start to look like a bad Italian restaurant!

Materials: stencils, sponge applicator, painter's tape, paint(s), and glaze(s)

How to: Tape your stencil to the surface—take care to consider architectural features or furniture when stenciling on a fixed surface such as a wall. Using the sponge applicator, simply apply as many layers of paint or glaze within the stencil as are necessary to make the paint look right. Don't remove the stencil between layers of paint, or you may not be able to replace it exactly over the first coat. Regal damask, Greek key borders, and small geometric shapes for patterning are my staple stencils, but I like to mix it up with larger, bolder ones that I come across all the time.

OTHER ESSENTIAL DIY TECHNIQUES

Upholstering

The Feeling: Upholstering adds substance to a surface and brings out the texture of the material used. Upholstered panels on walls are a fantastic way to bring an uncanny, even exotic look to a room. Old furniture can be revitalized by upholstering sections of it—such as the arms and seat of an old wood chair.

Materials: fabric (textile, leather, faux leather, etc.), MDF, cotton batting, staple gun

How to: Though I use the example of MDF here, you can upholster directly to any wood surface that you can staple into (the arm or back of a chair, for example). That said, I advise starting with a test piece of MDF if you've never upholstered before so you have an idea of what a certain amount of batting will look like in a finished product. If your goal is to upholster a section of MDF to serve as a seat for a custom bench, let's say, then measure out enough fabric to wrap the showing side of the MDF and have plenty underneath it to spare—keep in mind that stuffing the fabric will require extra length and width in your measurements. Along one edge of the MDF and around the corners from that edge, staple the edges of the fabric to the bottom side. You should now have a sort of sleeve into which you can stuff cotton batting and staple up the sides as you go. Attach the upholstered panel with hot glue, mounting hooks, tacks, or nails.

I HAVE ALMOST ALL OF THE ESSENTIALS IN MY LOFT SPACE

VENETIAN PLASTER ✳

✳ WOOD-GRAINING BEAM

STENCIL ON ✳ WALL

UPHOLSTERED LEATHER ✳ CHAIR

PART ONE

THE BLUEPRINT

The Foundation of

High-Style, Low-Cost Decorating

CHAPTER ONE

HIGH-STYLE, LOW-COST PRINCIPLES OF PLANNING

Frank's Plan for Creating Beauty on a Budget

It's no secret that a well-designed space, even on a budget, consists of a few basic components that most of us already know about, such as color, layout, furniture, and accessories. I'll be talking about those soon, and these are important elements of a room's style, but they are only tools that serve as *your* designated goals.

At this point, I want to double-check that you have started with my Q.D.E. basics. Function, ambiance, and cohesion—those have all undergone due consideration, right? Good. That's the Q.D.E. enhanced version of the daydreaming that you've been doing as you grew more and more excited about revamping your home. Now it's time to take the logistics into account. In this chapter, I'll break down everything you need to prepare for, and how to do just that: prepare. Just as having a design in mind is the best way to bring your ideal space into being, having a plan lined up is the number one way to make sure this whole process costs as little time and money as possible.

Speaking of plans . . . care to know an industry secret? I don't mean a secret just from my time as a professional decorator, but especially from my time as a television design show host. You do? Here it is: WE DO NOT just show up at our guest's door and shout "Hooray for you! You're getting a home makeover!" Well, we do this at some point—you've seen it. But we designers meet with our guests before the cameras come out. We talk to people about their overall likes and dislikes to gain a feel for their personalities. We discuss color loves and color fears. We talk about sports teams, old pets, and high school crushes . . . okay, maybe I'm exaggerating a bit. Still, we try to learn as much as we can before we shout "Lights, camera, action!" We, in the design-show business, have some of the tightest budgets imaginable. My show, which is about designing on a low budget, may be the most restrictive of them all. This doesn't mean I sacrifice results, but it does mean I do plenty of planning.

Remember: No shopping until you've read through the following list and made a plan!

Follow these ten steps to formulate and develop your design plan.

1. Create an Inspiration Folder

Look for finished looks that you love. You're not going to copy these room for room—that would be like buying your whole décor in one set from a design store—but you're certainly going to go to school on them. Pablo Picasso once said, "Bad artists copy. Good artists steal." Keeping that in mind, try to steal from the best rooms you see without fully copying them. Gather magazine clippings, fabric samples, paint chips, etc., that represent the design elements you would like to use in your home. Scour your favorite design magazines and furniture catalogs for the most current looks. Go to your local fabric and paint stores for swatches. Many times I have found inspiration in TV and movies, so ready your DVRs so you can play back your favorite scenes. Be conscious of the Q.D.E. vision you have during your search, but don't be overly strict—allow your vision to respond to your findings.

2. Create a Realistic Budget

Time for your first reality check. Don't worry, you won't have to make as many sacrifices to style as you think. For now, though, decide on a cap. The biggest things to factor in are those new purchases you know you need to make. You're probably not going to build a bed or a couch or a new countertop yourself, so if that needs doing, you need to account for it. Other than that, we're going to be really thrifty. The goal here is an absolute limit on what you can spend. No matter what that is, I'll help you make it work. Without a limit, decorating projects can spiral way out of control, so this is an important step.

After deciding on a ceiling number, set up a sheet with columns to track your spending. Note what is returnable—you don't want to finish everything and find that the most expensive piece you bought doesn't belong in the room you created. Keep all your receipts from the project in the same place.

DIRTY LITTLE SECRET

WATCH FOR THE "LOOK FOR LESS" TECHNIQUES

Find a high-ticket inspiration item that you would love to have in the room, but don't buy it. Study its lines, details, and materials. Then hit thrift stores and hotel resellers to look for the closest match that fits in your budget.

3. Determine Your Design Style

All too often, people head into a home makeover without fully understanding one of the most important aspects of any interior designer's job: knowing your design style. A thorough understanding of your design style, from its history to its evolution in today's design world, can save you from making the wrong investments. A chosen style, even allowing for deviation, will inform all of your purchases, from the major new items through the colors and down to those pesky brass tacks. Let your home's existing architecture, your cultural upbringing, and your likes and dislikes factor into deciding what design style works for you. To further help you determine your style, stop and ask yourself: *What the heck do I really want anyway?* I'll provide a detailed aid for answering that question in Chapter Two.

DIRTY LITTLE SECRET

IT'S ECLECTIC!

If you're commitment-phobic or just love too many styles to choose one, then create your own. Call it "eclectic," and be sure to keep some cohesiveness with your colors, wood tones, and fabric choices. Most importantly . . . OWN IT!

4. Consider Scale

Scale refers to the size of the architectural features of a space as well as the height, width, depth, and length of furnishings, artwork, and accessories in your room. When scale is off, you will get a room that feels chaotic and looks unbalanced. Scale is very often that unnamable thing that people don't like about otherwise nice spaces. My rule of thumb is that large rooms should generally be furnished by larger items. Towering armoires, over-sized sofas, floor-to-ceiling drapes, and big dramatic chandeliers are examples of different objects you can use to put a large room into perspective. If you have a small space, create the illusion of height with short, multipurpose furnishings.

DIRTY LITTLE SECRET

THE ROOM REVOLVES AROUND YOU

Scale also revolves around your own personal size—if you are a tall person, you will want furnishings that won't make you feel cramped, and if you are of shorter stature, you will want furnishings that don't overpower you.

5. Create a Furniture Inventory

Figure out what belongs in a room by evaluating your furniture, and put each piece into simple categories like seating, surfaces, and storage. Have some sense about this: A couch counts more toward seating than a single chair, for instance. The main criteria here are what is needed and what fits. The secret is finding that balance between the different furnishings and decorations you already own and the new pieces you might want to bring into a room. You literally earn bonus points for furniture with multiple functions; an ottoman that doubles as a chest scores for both seating and storage. Don't think that multipurpose furniture automatically frees you up to buy one more piece, either—open space adds to a room and not to your budget.

KICK OUT THE HANGERS-ON

I have literally been in hundreds of homes, and it's inevitable: Somewhere in the home you can find a hideous futon, halogen lamp, or other item leftover from someone's college days. Think of a before-and-after picture of your room makeover that rids you of these impersonal, standard-issue items.

6. Keep an Uncluttered Perspective

Now that you know what you need, it's time to ditch what you don't! Purge and de-clutter! Sell things, and if you can't, then give them to friends, charity, and the Dumpster. If you think you might use something in the new space, save it only after trying once more to toss it (test your commitment!). Cramming too much furniture or too many accessories and knick-knacks into a room complicates scale and detracts from a feeling of openness. Try to pare down to one or two large, bold pieces of art and lay off the little stuff. Allow colors and texture to speak for the design instead of trying to add too many accessories in an attempt to portray a certain style.

TIPS FOR CHOOSING ART AND ACCESSORIES

* Look for meaningful pieces that tell your story.
* Use discretion—not every surface has to be covered.
* Don't be an overzealous accessory queen or king.
* For dramatic effect, choose wall art that is large in scale.

7. Draw a Floor Plan

Remember that vision you either had in your head or drew out after fitting your design to my Q.D.E.? Whether you had a mass of mental squiggles or you broke out the ol' protractor, it's time for a major revision to the sketch. Take measuring tape to everything: walls, doorways, windows, architectural features, and furniture. Draw with a ruler and an easy measurement reference, like an inch equals a foot (and use a pencil, *fear the pen!*). Ask yourself whether the sketch, as it is now, is harmonious with your original Q.D.E. vision and its distributions of matter and presence. If not, are the changes for the better? Feel free to label out the centers of ambiance so you can confirm that everything is still underpinned by the Q.D.E. If you find you have a hand for sketching, try zeroing in on the most ambient areas and fine tune them with measurements. Try to create vignettes and groupings of seating with furniture that provide additional conversation areas and divide the room in a pleasing way.

WORK WITH ONE SMALL SPACE AT A TIME

Try to create vignettes and groupings of seating with furniture that provide additional conversation areas and help break up your room. Don't just throw a comfy sofa in a room next to the hand-me-down coffee table and call it a day; it will feel empty.

8. The Final Function Check

After verifying that the unity and uniqueness of your ambiance is still intact, go back to the room's purpose. It should still be served with no degraded convenience and lots of new style.

To help you define the function of each room in your home, ask yourself the following questions that I ask my clients the first time we meet and discuss their decorating dilemma:

* Will this room serve you for the whole time you stay in your current home?
* Will the space stand up to your and your family's lifestyle?
* Does the design scheme enhance, not interfere with, the activities the room will host?
* Do you have enough storage?

If each of those questions is answered with a confident "Yes!" then congratulations are in order, because you've brought your vision through the planning needed to make it all happen for as little money as possible. If not, don't fret. Use that eraser and rearrange things, or cut them out completely, to facilitate function and flow.

9. Create a Work Flow and Schedule

It is important to list what you will be doing and when you intend on doing it. Try to prioritize projects in order of the workload required and how much time you need based on your skill level and your availability. But before you book yourself completely, give some thought to the major saver of money and maker of style that is the tenth step:

My Space

Create a space in your home that is yours and yours alone. This space should be a reprieve from the trappings of modern life. Whether you use it to meditate, read, journal, or listen to soothing music, reserve this space as a sanctuary for your time. Take haven here at least once a week to check in with yourself without the interruption of cell phones, TV, etc. Without your sense of personal balance and well-being, you can't truly function with clarity and power in the real world. Creating a place that is all about you will make you feel energized and creative again! (Candles and aromatherapy optional.)

Let your imagination run wild when designing your personal sanctuary. I've seen people with spaces so unique that they transform the feel of the entire house. Adding a niche dedicated to you is the easiest way to change a house into a home. My friend Marty Dunne's home has one of my favorite examples. Some folks are cat people, some dog people . . . Marty is a bird guy. Using small potted trees, wood chips, and stones, he turned his basement into a small aviary for his several birds. Now whenever he needs to forget the outside world, he walks downstairs into a colorful, chirping forest.

You don't need the space or collection of tropical birds that Marty does to carve out a personalized haven. What you should copy, however, is his willingness to dream big about what makes him happy and not limit yourself to typical design items.

10. DIY (Do It Yourself) Saves Dough

Time to get hands-on! Before you start swinging the hammer, first know your comfort zone. You need to be honest about your skill level and be real about what you're capable of in terms of availability to commit to a project, skill level, and finances. Luckily, you have this book, which I've filled with DIY projects for the builder on a budget. All of them are customizable to fit your personality and design style, and they will all yield pieces that will look just as good as what you can buy at the design store . . . plus they're 100 percent original.

Trust me, I've worked with customers both on screen and off, and I know that even the most inept-seeming person can become a DIY pro with the right instruction.

Life, like a great design, is always a work in progress. The willingness to change, adapt, and try new things is necessary for success. Rough economies are perfect examples of how we must adapt to change. I am challenged daily to shop, build, refurbish, and paint with just pennies and pure creativity. Now you're armed with my methods and your own plan. The upcoming chapters will break down more of my tricks, tips, and Dirty Little Secrets, project by project, room by room. Living with high style without draining your bank account is possible—let's get started!

PUTTING IT ALL TOGETHER
cohesion

Whenever you are at loss in determining the design for the space you are redecorating, refer back to these steps. Your inspiration folder should be the first destination, then consider reexamining your layout and how the scale of everything will balance when arranged according to your floor plan. Before you add new items, remember that you don't want to clutter the space. Before you purchase something new, consider DIY projects to change existing items or build new ones for less money than a new purchase. The last step you should return to should be number two; the other steps will offer you new changes so you won't have to expand your budget.

CHAPTER TWO

KNOW YOUR DESIGN STYLE

Learn the Language of Design to Help You Save a Dime

There is a downside to the huge amount of home design stores and brands that have really boomed in recent years. They tend to provide too many choices for us. Sure, you can choose couch A over couches B and C in a catalog, but really there are *so many more* choices out there! Flea markets, online buying, repurposing what you have—the cheaper ways to buy items for your space yield much more variety than any catalog. The knowledge that can broaden your options, which home design companies have and use to make decisions for us, is a knowledge of design styles. Design styles are categories that every item you will put in your home can be classified into.

Think about it in terms of clothes: When you get dressed or go shopping, you know what general look you're trying to establish. You look for items that align to a style (for example: professional, preppy, old-fashioned Hollywood, hip-hop, high fashion, and many others) and, obviously, you have an idea of what fits the style of an outfit and what doesn't. Home design styles work exactly the same way—they might even be more concretely defined than fashion categories.

So having a design style in mind for a room helps you make decisions when shopping, decorating, and making DIY items. It's *way* better to go through the decorating process knowing (and this is just one example) "I want things that fit an Arts and Crafts style," instead of thinking "I want stuff that looks like it came out of West Elm's catalog." I have nothing against West Elm, but knowing your design style is the best way to achieve a more original look on a smaller budget. Like in clothing fashion, you can have one or two pieces from a top brand and then, because you know your style, fill the rest of the outfit out from affordable stores. Knowledge is the power to save major cash!

TRUE CONFESSIONS

One of the first things I do in preparing for episodes, and probably one of the easiest ways for me to figure out a *Design on a Dime* guest's preferences, is to ask them about design styles. Many people know a few (Traditional, Modern) but people who don't decorate for a living can't usually list the intricate differences between Romantic and Neo-Classical décor.

On *Design on a Dime* or most any TV design show I've ever worked on, we have something called "pre-shoot scouts." This is basically the window of opportunity for the homeowner to speak freely about what type of make-over they might want or expect, as well as a reality check that you're about to be on national television! This time is also an opportunity for producers to find storylines and for me to get a feel for my new client. I once walked into a pre-shoot scout meeting, with a room full of producers, design assistants, and one homeowner who after ten minutes came to tears because she didn't know her design style. I kid you not. Maybe it was the pressure of all the people in the room mixed with a little stage fright. I took her by the hand and assured her that I wouldn't sleep until I found her design style.

What I do with guests is sit them down, ask them the general vibe they like (in terms of time period, places they have visited, shapes, and colors), and then use pictures and descriptions to walk them through the essentials of the design styles that might fit their taste. From there it's easy to ask them for two or three design styles they want me to draw on, and it's a guarantee that they'll like the end product. This chapter is a compendium of the most common design styles and the defining characteristics of each. Once you have a proper name of a style in mind, you can ask at most stores you go to (many thrift stores and flea markets, too) and locate your best options with ease.

A COMMON PROBLEM: FEELING TRAPPED

But what if you're shopping around and find an item that is completely to die for but doesn't fit your chosen design style? *And* it's on sale!? Well, you need to think for a moment. Furniture (for example) is not an item you want to make an impulse purchase on. The reality is this: As cheap or great as this item is, it will not look as good in a room that doesn't complement its style as it would in a room that aligns with it. If you absolutely must have it, one option is to let this item be your single "clash piece." A room that is 95 percent one style and 5 percent another can be very bold and chic as long as

WHEN WORKING WITH WOOD. . .

Many design styles will call for lots of wood furnishings. Avoiding buying a set of furniture or décor is a great way to save money and stay original, but that means you need to have an eye for matching distinct items. When purchasing wood furnishings, a good rule of thumb is to not have the color of all the wooden items in a space differ by more than three shades. If you absolutely love a piece but it is too dark or light, you can always sand it and add a new finish.

FRAME IS DARK WOOD *

HUTCH IS * MEDIUM WOOD

* FLOOR IS SLIGHTLY LIGHTER COLOR

there is a good story to tell about the piece or it serves an amazingly unique function. Make it belong to your design. In the end, you need to make a call based on your gut feeling and better judgment. There are design styles that simply don't work together. A room decked out in modern metal furniture and décor with one ornately carved wood baroque end table will generally not look good, because the styles are too far apart. Make judgment calls based on time period, geography, and color scheme to determine whether two items from different styles can work together. Consider their stories: Neo-Classical and Mediterranean styles are quite different, but ultimately Neo-Classicism is rooted in Ancient Greece and Rome, and those were Mediterranean civilizations—both styles have a Mediterranean element—so the clash can connect.

Knowing the design style of the piece you want can also allow you to change your whole design style plan if you want to.

FRANK'S DICTIONARY OF DESIGN STYLES

Without further ado, here are the design style categories that all furniture and décor you may find will fit into.

Q.D.E. ALERT
ambiance

Obviously your chosen design style will strongly impact your space's ambiance: It dictates what most of the décor looks like! When determining whether to break or bend a style, consider the story of the ambiance as a whole. Putting two items together that were manufactured at the same time, even if in different places and after different styles, can tell an interesting story. Knowing the story of your décor will also allow you to fit collectables or heirlooms that you thought might not have made the cut before, thus adding to the overall ambiance.

Art Deco

This geometric, dramatic style dominated American cities in the first half of the twentieth century. Think of the big, lavish world of millionaires, mobsters, and theaters in the golden age. The buildings Batman perches on as he watches the streets of Gotham City for crime are Art Deco emblems. This look can be had for cheap by using lots of metallic faux finishes!

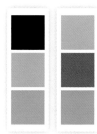

MATERIALS:
Chrome, dark lacquered woods, pewter, glass, mirrors, leather, velvet

SHAPE:
Sleek lines, sometimes with dramatic vertical curves

COLOR:
Cooler and metallic; glossy is good; dim lighting

TIME/PLACE:
New York, Chicago, and Miami, peaking in the 1930s and '40s.

IN THE WORLD:
The Empire State Building, Tony Montana's digs in *Scarface*

TELLTALE DÉCOR TO SEE IF YOU'RE SHOPPING IN THE RIGHT DIRECTION:

ARTS AND CRAFTS (MISSION STYLE)

This style glorified hand craftsmanship and natural simplicity. Exposed joinery and spare ornamentation that lets the shape of an item do the talking is popular. Colors should be either natural or reflect the subtlety of non-tropical nature. The tone is strong, raw, and handsome with an inherent elegance. The seeds of the movement were a reaction against mass production in favor of personalized design.

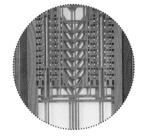

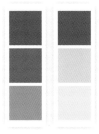

MATERIALS:
Dulled metals, stained or blown glass, painted tile, stenciled and hand-dyed cloth

SHAPE:
Simple and angular shapes; furniture shows how it was put together

COLOR:
Dusty and muted hues; no bright primary colors

TIME/PLACE:
1910–1925 in the United States and late nineteenth century in Britain

IN THE WORLD:
California bungalow homes

TELLTALE DÉCOR TO SEE IF YOU'RE SHOPPING IN THE RIGHT DIRECTION:

Asian

Mostly drawing from China and Japan, Asian décor utilizes raw materials, sophisticated finishes, and traditional stenciling to create a serene representation of the natural world. Floral shapes and graceful lines are often subtly present. Stencils in black ink with pale highlights can enhance an Asian mood.

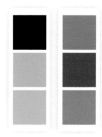

MATERIALS:

Raw materials like bamboo, rattan, and stone

SHAPE:

A combination of straight and round shapes; edges often curve but not intrusively

COLOR:

Anything found in nature—the brightest tend to come from flowers

TIME/PLACE:

Feudal Japan is most iconic (think of the films of Akira Kurosawa), but the style has persisted for centuries

IN THE WORLD:

Pagodas are major architectural examples

TELLTALE DÉCOR TO SEE IF YOU'RE SHOPPING IN THE RIGHT DIRECTION:

Contemporary

This style has roots in Modernism but softens the lines and incorporates elements from more traditional design styles in an original way. Contemporary rooms offer a hip vibe while looking highly comfortable at the same time.

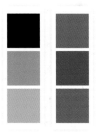

MATERIALS:
Metal and thick, independently structured upholstery

SHAPE:
Round, ergonomic lines meant to beckon you to relax while glowing with style. The lines are not nearly as rigid as in Modern décor

COLOR:
Rich and deep tones of bronze, purple, burnt orange, caramel, gold, black, and brown

TIME/PLACE:
Metropolitan America after the 1980s with a Scandinavian influence

IN THE WORLD:
Lofts in large cities often look to contemporary style

TELLTALE DÉCOR TO SEE IF YOU'RE SHOPPING IN THE RIGHT DIRECTION:

Country Cottage

A colorful, comfortable American style with painted and/or decorated furniture with plenty of beveling. Weathered finishes are not uncommon, though usually specific textures and colors vary depending on geographical settings (tune into the colors of your region's natural features). The general setting is great for mixing up some lemonade or brewing a pot of tea.

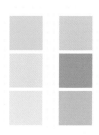

MATERIALS:
Light wood; slim wrought iron in the outdoors

SHAPE:
Curved and beveled furniture limbs and comfortably arched seat backs

COLOR:
Plenty of whitewashing with pale or muted pastels

TIME/PLACE:
Rural American towns in the early to mid-twentieth century

IN THE WORLD:
Small-town homes in *Fried Green Tomatoes* or a luxurious version in *Gone with the Wind*

TELLTALE DÉCOR TO SEE IF YOU'RE SHOPPING IN THE RIGHT DIRECTION:

Global Eclectic

The look of a world traveler's home. Variety is key, but make sure you find furnishings that express exciting foreign cultures. This is a more free version of the older British Colonial look—no need to draw exclusively from the old British Empire. Plain furniture can be converted to fit this style by using an exciting faux wood-grain finish.

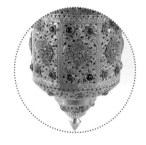

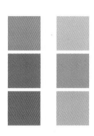

MATERIALS:

Lots of medium to dark wood, either raw or lacquered

SHAPE:

Usually ornamented shapes that don't need to be similar except in that they are from another time or place

COLOR:

An earth-based palette of burnt reds, washed-out blues, yellows, oranges, and wooded browns

TIME/PLACE:

The Age of Exploration or your dream travel destinations

IN THE WORLD:

When faced with a decision think, "Would Ernest Hemingway have decorated with this?"

TELLTALE DÉCOR TO SEE IF YOU'RE SHOPPING IN THE RIGHT DIRECTION:

Hollywood Regency

This style sports an overtone of vintage glitz and glamour that is often complemented with Asian accents. Though its roots are in the Golden Era of Hollywood (the heyday of Gary Cooper, Marlene Dietrich, Clark Gable, and Ginger Rogers) it has come back with renewed style and affordable updates in recent years. Graphic, bold contrast is what this style is all about.

MATERIALS:

Wood painted in vibrant colors and upholstering with exotic patterns

SHAPE:

Ornamented curves without as much beveling as more traditional styles; upholstering should not be too bulky

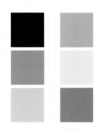

COLOR:

Graphic colors like yellow, black, Kelly green, and orange

TIME/PLACE:

Where Bugsy Siegel and Frank Sinatra sipped martinis

IN THE WORLD:

The Hollywood Hills haven't forgotten this style, but it is often adjusted in chic houses all over the country with a slight change of color palette

TELLTALE DÉCOR TO SEE IF YOU'RE SHOPPING IN THE RIGHT DIRECTION:

Modern

Modern design changed the game when it came from Europe to America around the middle of the century. It reached peak popularity in the 1960s and held strong until the '80s. Modern decorating is the opposite of Traditional. It abandons opulence in favor of a minimalist merger of form and function. The overall sense of cohesion in Modern rooms is impressive, and designers love to come up with incredible new ways to work with the simple, straight-lined forms that this style calls for. This style is both simple and futuristic.

MATERIALS:
Metal, glass, and plastic with low-profile upholstery

SHAPE:
Straight and clean; curved lines usually only come in to soften transitions in furniture

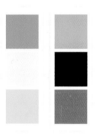

COLOR:
Black and white are the bases, but the central shades of colors like red, yellow, orange, and green are often used as highlights

TIME/PLACE:
The time in the mid-twentieth century when everyone was getting excited about all the flying cars we would have in the year 2000

IN THE WORLD:
Movies set in the future often employ modern décor. Also, the Malibu home of Robert Downey Jr. as Tony Stark in *Ironman* is an excellent example

TELLTALE DÉCOR TO SEE IF YOU'RE SHOPPING IN THE RIGHT DIRECTION:

TRADITIONAL

Traditional style is the dominant high-class style of eighteenth-and nineteenth-century Europe and America. Embroidery and ornamented wood and metal shapes form the basis of this highly elegant style. Curtains, throws, and rugs should lay on the luxury. Traditional décor is the opposite of Modernism.

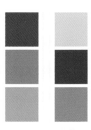

MATERIALS:
Embroidered fabric upholstery, classy dulled metal, and dark wood (Wood graining and metallic faux finishes are excellent to turn used furniture into high-class traditional fare!)

SHAPE:
Plenty of arches and long curves with floral embellishment; clawed furniture feet is a classic element

COLOR:
Golds, browns, wheat, creams, burgundy, and some blues give a neutral, classy, and regal feel, with the occasional colonial red for contrast

TIME/PLACE:
High-class Europe for the past few centuries and throughout the history of America with a several decades' lull after American Independence

IN THE WORLD:
Martin Scorsese's *Age of Innocence* is among the best representations of classic Traditional décor in cinema

TELLTALE DÉCOR TO SEE IF YOU'RE SHOPPING IN THE RIGHT DIRECTION:

EVEN MORE DESIGN STYLES

So far I've introduced the most common design styles—furnishing usually matches up with one of the prior categories. The remaining descriptions in the dictionary are more brief but should give you a good idea of what the remaining style categories are like. If you ask for items in any of the styles listed, a clerk or manager should know what you're looking for. If they don't, then now you can tell them—don't be surprised if you walk out with both a beautiful item and a job offer!

Baroque

This highly ornamental decorative style originated in Italy in the 1600s. It is characterized by twisted columns, large irregular curves, large surfaces, oversize moldings with scrollwork, luxurious fabrics, and inlaid wood floor designs. Gold is the predominant color and is supported with strong hues like purple, dark green, deep red, and burnt umber for a rich, regal look. Lighting is often dimmed to bring out shadow contrast.

British Colonial

Spurred by the arrival of the British colonists in the West Indies, this style represents a combination of pared-down Victorian elegance with tropical plant and animal motifs. Furniture usually consists of mahogany, dark walnut, or teak combined with wicker, cane, and leather insets. Finishes are minimal and almost never glossy.

Eclectic

Eclectic style encompasses a variety of periods and styles and relies on the use of color, texture, shape, and finish to provide cohesion.

French Provincial / French Country

Rustic versions of formal French furnishings of the 1600 and 1700s, such as the Louis XIV and Louis XV styles, are typical French Provincial / French Country. (Regal French styling like that at Versailles went out of style quickly because of its extreme cost.) Early French Country pieces were considered peasant furniture. Typical colors used are Mediterranean blue, sunny yellow, terra-cotta red, and green. Natural materials like stone and terra-cotta are used abundantly in addition to wire and wrought iron.

Lodge

A look characterized by natural materials like leather, wool, and indigenous woods from the area. The key is to keep everything in a rustic state. Décor is usually large, abundant, and characteristic of the local area.

Mediterranean

This style hails from Spain, Greece, and Italy. Walls are predominantly textured with plaster or tile. (Faux texturing is the best way to achieve a gorgeous Mediterranean look!) This style will help guests dream of a villa in Ibiza, a home on the winding streets of Athens, or dinner in the Italian countryside. The combination of rustic and luxe in the Mediterranean style is tough to beat!

Mid-Century Modern

Mid-Century Modern was created from the 1930s to 1970s. It overlapped in time with Modernism but attempted to be the colorful sibling. The look is comprised of accessories in organic shapes, clean lines, flat-painted walls, and bent plywood frames used for furnishings. The use of wood and wood veneer in the face of Modernism's rejection of wood was an important difference. Other materials were developed and used during the period, including colorful plastics, vinyl, melamine, and formica. Lighting became an artistic statement, with pieces featuring floating circles, triangles, cones, and radiant arms made out of steel, brass, and aluminum with brightly colored shades. If you're going for a retro look, Mid-Century Modern is a great place to start.

Moroccan

A detailed look consisting of intricately patterned fabrics, colorful mosaics, metal lanterns, textured walls, gauzy fabric, jewel-toned colors, layers of Oriental rugs, pillows in luxurious fabrics, and ornately carved wooden accents. Basically, Morocco knows how to do luxury. Fabrics are key here, and the look can be made for cheap by using printed throws and drapes in combination with metallic faux finishes, stenciling, and polished stone effects.

Neo-Classical

Neo Classical décor is an elegant and simple design style, with motifs borrowed from ancient Roman, Greek, and Egyptian themes. Originating as part of the larger Neo-Classical movement that began in the mid-to late eighteenth century, Neo-Classical furniture typically features a restrained symmetrical design with distinctive geometrical shapes and fluted references to the classical architectural columns of ancient Greece. Stenciling is a great way to highlight Neo-Classical motifs in your space.

Old World

The hallmark of Old World design is a comfortable, broken-in look that shows the wear and tear of use. Textured walls, hand-trawled windows and walls, and natural materials like tumbled marble exemplify the style. Wood surfaces are often rather heavy. The finish of the materials is extremely important—distressed furniture and matte finishes are preferable to highly polished, reflective surfaces. Don't be afraid to break out the sandpaper to dull wood that is too glossy. Colors are muted and subdued.

Rococo

A style of European design originating in France during the early 1700s and featuring furniture made of rich woods with elaborate scrollwork and curved forms. It's considered a more refined version of the coarse and heavy Baroque style. Colors and lighting can all be light and pale, but a few dominant colors can be bright and bold.

Romantic

A comfortable style that appeals to the senses with soft fabrics with floral patterns, laces, painted furniture, pastels, filtered light, and aromatic flower arrangements. Color splashes and stenciling will help highlight the Romantic tone, especially if you don't have much artwork to hang. But don't shy away from framing prints!

Rustic

Regardless of your home's location, Rustic styling is a simple mode typical of country life. Interiors are primitive with exposed brick walls, wood paneling, rough-hewn beams, and stone. Furnishings are simple yet

A SLEEK BEDROOM THAT SCREAMS MID-CENTURY MODERN CLASS *

sturdy pieces with little ornamentation and natural or worn finishes. Color tends not to be bright, but a wide variety can be used.

Shabby Chic

This style has become popular in recent years because of its variety and affordability. White-painted furniture, motifs of muted colors, slipcovers, and vintage fabrics are all indicative of this comfortable, eclectic look. People often put a "garden" twist on Shabby Chic décor by adding floral themes, needlepoint pillows, lace accents, and fresh flowers.

Southwestern

Southwestern is generally characterized by earth-tone colors, rough textures, handcrafted objects, and an abundance of terra-cotta and clay-tile roofs. This stems from Mexico and is often given a hint of cowboy flair. Try some plaster tinted with earth and desert tones and see how Southwestern your space immediately feels!

Transitional

Transitional style is a marriage of traditional and contemporary furniture, finishes, materials, and fabrics. Furniture lines are either straight or rounded. Fabric can range from graphic patterns on overstuffed sofas to textured chenille on sleek wood frames. Transitional décor can be more whimsical than Contemporary or sparse Modern furnishings. Faux metallic finishes and stencils can help blur the lines between Modern and Traditional.

Tropical

Ornamental carvings in island motifs, exotic woods, and framed botanical drawings are indicative of this style. Light and airy textiles such as burlap, organza, and linen are often used. Patterns of tropical plants and trees can be used in upholstery, throws, and pillows. Color splashes and faux finishes can really bring this look home.

Tudor

Tudor is a highly decorated style that was in effect from 1485 to the death of Queen Elizabeth in 1603. It signaled the transition from Medieval to Renaissance design with stone or brick floors, contrasting colors, and ornate

furniture. Pewter accessories are plentiful. The look depends on a recurrent use of textural fabrics on beds, windows, and walls. Textured plaster finishes can help add to the vibe.

Tuscan

Tuscan interiors are similar to Mediterranean spaces but feature a more rustic, sun-baked look characterized by crumbling stone, simple and sturdy furnishings with iron accents, terra-cotta tiles, and textured wall finishes. Elegant, detailed murals and trompe l'oeil ("trick of the eye") designs can be alluded to with carefully chosen stenciling.

Victorian

A style of furniture and architecture named for England's Queen Victoria that was very popular through the latter half of the nineteenth century, highlighted with elaborate carved floral designs. It is more embellished than straight Traditional style. Common elements of Victorian style include oval chair backs, marble tops on tables and dressers, fabrics and wall coverings featuring bold patterns in strong colors and draperies, and upholstered pieces embellished with extensive trimmings and fringe.

PUTTING IT ALL TOGETHER
cohesion

I know this might be difficult to hear, but a design style is all about commitment. Limiting yourself to no more than three styles in one space—and one tends to be ideal—is the most important thing you can do to enhance the cohesive feeling of your space. When the story of everything is closer together, it allows objects to add to each other's story in meaningful ways. Possibly the best part about knowing your design style is that it will make you a smarter shopper in the future: You'll know if an item is worth buying if it aligns to your chosen design style, not just if it catches your eye. Design styles: the best protection from impulse buys!

CHAPTER THREE

WALLS OF WONDER

*Using Color, Texture, and More to Create
the Best Environment for Your Design*

Painting your walls is among the cheapest, easiest way to bring a sweeping change to your space. This means that when you're decorating on a budget, using wall color and texture to up the drama of your design is an opportunity I would advise you not to pass up. So, knowing that (you might want to sit down for this), I have to tell you right now that it's time to *ditch the all-white walls!* (And don't think off-white is any better—it's time to be brave, people!) White walls have a place, and some design styles (Shabby Chic and the starkest Modernism, for example) almost demand it, but the right dose of color simply brings more to a room than white. Much more.

I have designed for lots of powerful, successful, and intelligent individuals who make major business decisions every day, but making a decision about color leaves them stumped. I find it intriguing to encounter clients who have major issues choosing and committing to a color. People get truly scared at the prospect. If you're feeling the same way, don't worry. I can talk you through the change and tell you all the reasons why it's the right decision. Believe me—if I didn't have the ability to talk my clients through this trying time, then before and after pictures on *Design on a Dime* would not be nearly as exhilarating . . . they'd just be kind of off-white (cream at best).

In this chapter, I'll provide advice about using paint selection, painting techniques, wallpapering, and more to bring some much-needed wonder to your walls, no matter what space you are working in.

TRUE CONFESSIONS

Even the pros have difficulties picking paint color. Every TV designer I know has had that moment (often more than one), whether the camera is on or off, when we realize that we screwed up the color selection. We have to deal with it, though, and that's why it's so nice having interns. Stopping production to send runners back to the paint store in the middle of the filming day is rough. Film crews turn pretty vicious when they are an hour behind on their lunch break! A hungry cameraman is something I hope you never have to deal with—they get very grouchy. Fortunately, at least regarding painting your walls, you probably won't have to.

A COMMON PROBLEM: Don't Let Painting Be a Headache

Many inspired painting odysseys have been cut short by pure frustration. Colors and patterns aside, here is the rundown of the can't-miss basics when painting a room:

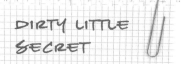

DIRTY LITTLE SECRET

DON'T BE AFRAID OF THE DO-OVER

It happens. You finish the first coat of a new color after priming and then it hits: You hate it. This is a part of the painting experience, and is not the fault of your taste. In fact, you have to always listen to your taste or your gut feeling, even when it tells you to go back to the color drawing board.

Changes in lighting between the paint store and your home are often the culprit in a color mishap such. Here's a way to help prevent the dreaded total do-over: Bring a color wheel or larger dry sample back to your home to examine it under the various conditions of your lighting. Do this before moving on to painting large sample swatches. This might save you a big step.

1. Dry work

Clear the room of furniture and décor. Sand and patch the walls. Remove all switch plates and outlet covers. Place the screws and plates into separate plastic bags and label the bags to remind you where they came from. I have lost plenty of those tiny screws, and I can tell you it ends up being easier and faster to remove, organize, and reinstall than putting them all in one heap. Tape any areas that need to be carefully trimmed, such as around windows, doors,

Q.D.E. ALERT
function

Your walls provide the environment for everything else in your rooms. They can function as so much more than the boundaries of a room—in fact, there is no limit to how much style they can add! Think of your walls as the best place to start laying the base of your room's style from color to texture and beyond.

and moldings. Cover the floors with old sheets or plastic drop cloths and tape these flush against the walls and exits of the room so no paint makes it to the floor. Know that step 1 can be a large chore! Consider doing it all the evening before you start to paint: Then you can start wielding those brushes with fresh energy in the morning.

2. Clean as you paint

Have paper towels and damp rags handy to grab any drips or spills as you go. Trust me, it happens to the best of us. Scrape globs or drips from windows, tile, or glass with straight razor blades. The good news is paint comes off those surfaces easier when dry, so continue painting, let the paint stiffen, and scrape later. If you're working over a rug that can't be rolled up, have a rug cleaning product handy.

3. Create a paint station

I can't tell you how many times I have found my foot on the upturned lid of a paint can as I stepped back to check my work. That's a liability. To avoid this messy step, open and store your paint cans on a drop cloth in the corner of a room and refill your paint trays at that location. Don't forget to cover your paint can quickly (no need to hammer them shut, just lay the covers on) between refills to keep the air out and your paint fresh.

4. Keep on rolling

There is a definite technique to rolling paint on your walls. After using the trimming brush near the ceilings, corners, and moldings, work your way across the walls with long,

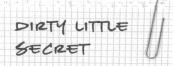

DIRTY LITTLE SECRET

THERE'S NO NEED TO FUMIGATE

If paint fumes bother you, try using low-VOC paint. (VOCs are Volatile Organic Compounds, and paints low in them are better for the environment and less harsh on your nose.) For a cheaper, home-grown solution, drop a few squirts of vanilla extract into the paint can, and breathe easier. (Note: The fumes are only masked, not eliminated.) It won't affect the color.

DIRTY LITTLE SECRET

GET YOUR OWN MAGIC WAND

This is one of the few places in this book I'll tell you to spring for something other than the most inexpensive option, but fortunately it's not even close to a budget-hog. Buy a substantial paintbrush and roller. For trim and corner painting you'll need a smaller brush that has an angular cut to the hairs. Your rollers need to be appropriate for your wall surface. If your wall (or ceiling) is porous or has texturing, you'll want to use a large-nap roller. Flat or smooth walls call for a low-nap roller. Also, cheap and disposable plastic liners for your paint trays make it easy to clean up and allow you to reuse the trays on another job.

As for overall quality, it's best to just ask. Any hardware store attendant will help you pick a good brush (if there's anyone left in this world you can trust not to pull one over on you, it's a hardware store manager).

broad, up-and-down rolls, overlapping each stroke by a few inches. Be sure the roller is fully covered with paint; dipping in the tray for each roll is better than dealing with inconsistencies in the coat.

5. Store wet brushes carefully while on breaks

Instead of washing your brush out each time you take a break, try wrapping your paint brush in plastic wrap or a plastic bag when you set it aside. You can even store it overnight if you keep it wrapped in plastic in the refrigerator.

6. Save your leftover paint

You might finish a job and a few weeks later notice a couple of scratches or other marks on the wall, but—*Oh no!*—you threw out your nasty, bulky paint cans. Avoid that headache by using resealable plastic containers or small glass jars with airtight lids to store paint you'll need for small touch-ups. Labeling them really helps too; be sure to put the color formula on the label in case you need to buy more paint.

MAKING THE LEAP TO A NEW WALL COLOR

Here are six common color issues people face when trying to choose a new color for their home:

1. GIVING IN TO THE FEAR OF COLOR.

Don't remain a color coward! The best way to get over that fear is to find a color that you love on a favorite item in your home. Look at an existing area rug, a painting, or a piece of fabric. If you like the color on items like these, you're more likely to like it on the walls. If the color you decide on is too strong, you don't need to abandon it. Try asking your paint store to formulate it at half-strength (and enjoy the impressed look on the paint mixer's face when you do so).

2. PUTTING TOO LITTLE COLOR ON THE WALLS

Look at your room in terms of the 60-30-10 rule that we designers employ: 60 percent of the color in a space comes from the walls; 30 percent from upholstery, floor covering, and window treatments; and 10 percent from accent pieces, accessories, and artwork. It's in the numbers: Liven up those white walls!

3. FORGETTING ABOUT PRIMER

Does the paint color at the store look rich and full until you put it on your wall, where it suddenly it looks completely different? If so, you forgot the primer. When changing the color of a wall, white or tinted primer is vital to achieving the actual color you picked out. Priming ensures that there will be no interference from the previous wall color. Using tinted primer that is close to your new wall color will save you time and money on a second or third coat of primer. But white primer is more universal, and you can use it if you decide to change your main color.

4. USING TOO MUCH OF A GOOD THING

Be aware of the intensity of the colors in a room. If you have a decorative area rug with five or six strong colors, don't paint the walls in equally strong hues. Let the rug be the focal point and paint the walls a lighter, complementary color. Furniture that is muted or monotone, however, can contrast nicely with bold wall colors.

5. RUSHING THE PROCESS

The best way to find a color you can live with is to paint a 4-foot-by-4-foot swatch (using cheap and sometimes free paint samples) on the wall and living with the color for 24 to 48 hours so you can see it in both natural daylight and artificial light. Being patient enough to take the extra time to do the swatch test is worth it to find a color you'll love living with for years. Just be sure you have some of the old wall color handy, just in case. Don't put the swatch in the middle of an open wall; try moving it slightly closer to a piece of cabinetry or furniture to better see how it will look in the context of the main wall and the room's other finished features.

6. NOT KNOWING THE FORMULA

Sometimes—and this is rare—a person goes through an honest effort to change the color of their walls and decides she just wants the old look back. If it's not too much trouble, figure out the formula of your starting color (this is why it's useful to save paint in the future). You know by now that I don't want you reverting to your old, white-walled ways, but people who know their formula can end up being more adventurous in their sampling—knowing you can return to exactly how things were provides a feel of comfort. Plus, after you have your stylish new color, you can go through the wonderful ritual of ripping the old formula to pieces!

ALTHOUGH TAN AND TAUPE CAN BE CALMING, TOO MANY MUTED NEUTRALS CAN ALSO BE A SNORE *

* A FEW GOOD PIECES OF COLORFUL ARTWORK CAN PUNCH UP THE EXCITEMENT

USING ARCHITECTURE TO HIGHLIGHT YOUR PAINT JOB

One of the most efficient ways to use color to transform a room is to play up your home's architectural features. Molding, mantels, coved or slanted ceiling-to-wall transitions, built-in bookcases, arched doorways, wainscot, windows, and even doors offer opportunities to add layers of interest and color. Painting the architectural features and keeping the walls white is also a way to add lots of noticeable color while keeping the walls basic.

An easy way to test the waters of architectural highlighting is by painting molding and doorway casings one step lighter or darker than the primary wall color. This can add cohesion and maturity to even the boldest paint jobs. This technique works with almost all design styles, from Pop-Art Modernism (I've seen an all hot-pink room that was made fully mature because of this technique) to classic Americana (think pale red walls and dark red architecture).

Anyone who watches HGTV knows I am a big fan of metallic paint! Finding an existing painted architectural element, like molding, wainscot, or a ceiling medallion and applying a metal glaze adds a regal feel to the space. Save this technique for simpler features: Built-in shelving and coved ceiling transitions are far bolder, and it's better to start with a simple shimmer first.

*LAYERED COPPER, GOLD, AND BRONZE METALLICS CREATE THIS GLOWING FAUX FINISH

Using an entirely different color for your architectural features is bolder but will yield super stylish results. Architectural elements can also provide cohesion throughout a house or series of rooms if they are painted the same color in each distinct space.

> Always defer to your instinct when you are combining colors. Use furniture, art, rugs, or combinations from the natural world to find sparks of inspiration.

Q.D.E. ALERT
ambiance

Color is central to a space's ambiance. If your walls pick up on the color themes of your room, it will make the overall unity of the space more complete. Pay attention to both the main and detail colors of the furniture and décor that you know will be in the room for a long time, and incorporate those colors into the paint scheme of the room. Make sure you are happy with how a color makes you feel, but don't be afraid to venture beyond your long-time favorites.

FINDING THE RIGHT COLOR PAIRINGS (OR TRILOGIES!)

There are so many resources to help you choose the right color combination. Most are based on the color wheel, which shows what colors harmonize so you don't have to. You can buy professional color wheels online for less than $10, which I recommend more than viewing one online because the lighting of your computer screen is very dishonest. Here are some of my favorite color combinations:

SAFE		BOLD	
⬤⬤⬤	Tan/White/Brown	⬤⬤⬤	Tan/Red/Black
⬤⬤⬤	White/Yellow/Peach	⬤⬤⬤	White/Black/Yellow
⬤⬤⬤	Blue/Cream/Yellow	⬤⬤⬤	Blue/Gold/White
⬤⬤⬤	Pink/Brown/Cream	⬤⬤⬤	Pink/Black/White

LOOK for LESS

DIY
PAPER BAG FAUX-LEATHER WALL TREATMENT

MATERIALS: brown paper grocery bags, polyurethane

TOOLS: paint roller, paintbrush

ASSEMBLY:

1. Tear the grocery bags into large pieces—try to keep each piece free of creases.
2. Roll a coat of polyurethane onto your surface (MDF is a good starter).
3. While the poly is wet, lay the paper pieces down with the blank side facing out. Let the edges overlap slightly.
4. Brush polyurethane over the paper in several coats. As it dries, the sheen will make the brown paper look like brown leather!

LOOK PAST PAINT: ALTERNATIVE WALL SOLUTIONS

Painting is not the only way to add color and style to your walls. Wallpaper, adhesive appliqués, and large-scale hangings will all bring dramatic changes to your walls without taking up extra space. The budget-friendly alternative surfacing technique closest to my heart is faux finishing, and this brings major character to walls. My favorite faux finishes for walls are a bright color wash, plaster texturing, metallic finishing for details, Venetian plaster, and wood graining for details; refer to the DIY Index, page 201, for the full how-to about faux finishing. Consider all the possible wall solutions as you plan your project and how you might want to combine them.

DIY

THE BEST FAUX FINISHES FOR YOUR WALLS

There is no limit to what you can do with your walls. If you consult my list of faux finishes on pages 12–14 then you'll soon find that price is not much of a limit either, if you use the right techniques. That said, here is a rundown of popular ways to use faux finishes on walls:

* **COLOR WASHING** is great for brightening up a whole wall or a section of it. Using an earth tone in a wash can also add an Old World, somewhat Tuscan look.

* **TEXTURING** with plaster is a technique that is easier and less expensive than you think. More rough applications with earth tone tints lend to an Old World look, whereas smooth applications with bold tints are more contemporary and even modern.

* **METALLIC PAINTS** are excellent as accents to a number of design styles depending on color and sheen.

CHAMPAGNE COLOR
METALLIC PAINT

* **POLISHED STONE / VENETIAN PLASTER** is a more regal look than texturing: Start with accents before attempting larger coverage.

* **WOOD GRAINING** is great for accents and faux wood elements like beams. (opposite)

* **STENCILING** is an amazing accent for adding a bold piece of artwork to a wall (or ceiling!) or a more subtle geometric pattern as trim.

COPPER
METALLIC
WALLPAPER

HERE, A DEEP RED
VENETIAN PLASTER AND
FAUX WOOD-GRAIN
BEAM CREATE A RUSTIC
VIBE. *

THE WONDERFUL WORLD OF WALLPAPER

Knowing the essential method for applying wallpaper will ensure that you don't end up with crooked patterns, air bubbles, or an overall mess.

1. THE RIGHT TOOLS

Make sure you have everything you need at your fingertips. Here is the basic kit you should always have with you when hanging wallpaper:

* pencil
* tape measure
* spirit level
* scissors
* paste bucket
* pasting brush
* a long, flat table
* seam roller
* smoothing brush
* sharp box cutter with plenty of extra blades

2. MATCH THE BATCH

When buying wallpaper, check to make sure the rolls have the same batch number. Color strength can vary from batch to batch, and you don't want mismatching walls.

3. PATTERN REPEATS

Before you start to measure and cut the wallpaper, check the label for pattern dimensions. Some wallpaper has a pattern that only matches at specific lengths. Make sure you cut each sheet as a multiple of the pattern repeat length (cut a pattern that repeats every 15 inches into 30-inch or 45-inch strips but not 40 inches).

4. KNOW THE LINGO

Match classifications will let you know how precise you have to be while cutting, measuring, and hanging. Most wallpaper will have instructions about how to match it.

* "Free match" is easiest to hang, and strips will always match up.
* "Straight match" means you need to match up the edges of the paper as you hang it horizontally.
* "Offset (or Drop) Match" requires some patience but can yield complex, gorgeous patterns. You tend to have to drop the strips by alternating distances as you go. The paper will provide specific symbols and instructions.

5. NEW TECHNOLOGY

"Paste the Wall" paper allows you to apply adhesive to the wall and stick the paper on without cutting the paper or needing a pasting table. The paper can easily be peeled off the wall at anytime by dragging it by the corner. This can save lots of time and costs the same as regular papers, though there is slightly less variety (for now).

DIY

BASKET-WEAVE PANELS FROM TOILET PAPER

MATERIALS: toilet paper (that's right), spray adhesive, brown and yellow glaze, polyurethane

TOOLS: soft paintbrush, stippling tool (a fork can work in a pinch), roller

ASSEMBLY:

1. Spray your surface (MDF is good for practice) with adhesive and lay toilet paper on in a cross-hatching basket pattern.
2. Using the brush and stippling tool, apply brown and yellow glazes until you like the color effect.
3. Roll a coat of polyurethane over the dried glazes to add a final sheen and protective seal.

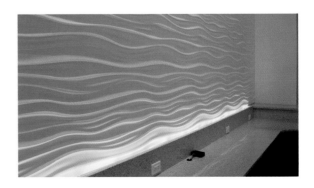

YOU CAN "PAINT" WITH LIGHT

Can't or won't paint your walls?
Looking for a way to vary a room's color depending on your mood? Try any of these four lighting effects to bring color and texture to your walls without the commitment and labor of painting. They are ranked by likely cost, #1 being most expensive.

1. GEL FILTERS

Take a cue from the world of photography and pick up a pack of colored lighting gels or filters. Having these thin plastic sheets handy can help change the atmosphere of a room by simply inserting a piece of the colored gel into an existing fixture or sconce. Under $20 for a multiple color pack.

2. FLOOR CAN LIGHTS

Hidden neatly behind a potted plant or a sofa, I suggest using a series of three evenly spaced floor cans to create a symmetrical and luminous effect along a wall. Use colored bulbs. For under $10 bucks a pop, that's a pretty cheap solution.

3. COLORED BULBS

The simplest way to add color for just a few dollars. They are likely to be less powerful than the previous two options. These bulbs come in almost any color for $2–$5, depending on wattage.

DIY

WALLPAPERING WITH FABRIC

MATERIALS: large section(s) of light-to medium-weight fabric, craft fabric starch

TOOLS: drop cloths, plastic bin or bathtub for soaking, razor or box cutter, straightedge

ASSEMBLY:

1. Purchase sections of fabric in strips as long as your wall's height and no wider than 3 feet. If you want to cover an area wider than 3 feet, use multiple strips.
2. Wash and dry all your sections of fabric before hanging so that any shrinkage will occur in advance.
3. In the tub or bin, follow mixing instructions for the craft starch. Soak each strip of fabric in the starch until saturated and bring it to the prepared hanging area.
4. Hang the fabric as you would hang wallpaper, flattening as you go. Allow a few inches of overlap at the ceiling and floor and between the separate strips of fabric.

Allow all hung fabric to dry, and then use the razor and straightedge to trim the excess at floor, ceiling, and between the fabric strips.

FAUX IT! ARCHITECTURAL FEATURES WITHOUT AN ARCHITECT

Not every home is decked out with fine architectural detail. Well, faux it then! The following DIY projects allow you to use paint in combination with cheap hardware store fare to style elements to your space that you may have thought impossible without a renovation.

DIY WORK YOUR OWN WAINSCOT

Wainscoting is a traditional design element originally meant to protect the lower third of a wall from dings and scratches that result from being at chair and child height. (Wainscoting usually starts 32 to 42 inches up from the floor or bottom edging.) Using various materials and paints, you can adapt wainscot to any design style and color scheme imaginable. Any hardware store clerk can guide you to the right materials if you ask for them by name. Following are some lower wall treatments I have used for years. If you're a renter or simply want to prevent serious mistakes and allow yourself to work in an area that's okay to get messy, I recommend applying treatments to thin sheets of plywood or MDF and then mounting the sheets to your wall with a drill and screws, then top that with cheap chair rail using finishing nails or caulk. As you use screws and nails in these projects, polish the look by sanding the wood over the nail, filling the depression caused by the nail with wood fill, and then sanding the wood fill after it dries and painting over it (unless you want a raw look like you might with the Country Eco-Chic wainscot). Make sure you use a level when mounting everything.

Tools:

hammer, hand saw, nails, wood fill, sandpaper, electric drill, screws, level

Island Bamboo

Materials: bamboo fencing, U-tacks

Assembly: Find some bamboo reed fencing at a large hardware store. Cut it down to the height and width needed using either a pair of wire snips or a small handsaw (tip: prevent the bamboo reeds from sliding around while you cut by taping the fence sections together just below where you cut, then gently remove once finished). Tack the fence to your wainscot area of the wall sheet using U-tacks. As a creative chair rail, I recommend screwing not one but two horizontal bamboo rods above the wainscot for a double dividing layer.

Art Deco

Materials: small MDF squares, fabric of choice, cotton batting, metallic painted wood chair rail

Tools: staple gun for fabric wrapping, picture hanging system or industrial Velcro or industrial adhesive of choice

Assembly: Find two types of shimmery or faux-leather fabric in a gray and black color. Have a hardware store cut as many ¼-inch thick MDF squares between a hand's height and a foot square as you need to cover your wainscot. Upholster these with a thin layer of cotton batting and the fabrics of your choice (be sure to leave a cleanly and flatly stapled fabric seam on the backside so your panel will be as flush to the wall as possible). Alternate individual squares (like a chessboard) or angle them in a slanted-diamond pattern (you'll have to cut partial squares at the corners of the wainscot if you choose to angle it). To mount the squares you can either use industrial Velcro, a hook-and-loop fastener, or a picture hanging hook system. Cap this it with a simple 1-inch by 3-inch chair rail with a metallic paint finish.

Colonial

Materials: eggshell raspberry or other similar dark-colored paint, white glossy paint, white beveled MDF chair rail

Tools: drop cloths, paint brush, hammer and nails, wood putty for filing nail holes

Assembly: This is pretty safe to put right on the wall. Paint the wainscoting area (approximately 36 inches high and however long your wall is) with a dark, classic paint (I like raspberry) for heavy contrast against the glossy white. Top this with a traditional white beveled MDF chair rail; add some vertical strips of chair rail about every 2½ feet across the wall for added interest.

Venetian

Materials: tinted plaster, pine chair rail, dark stain, iron nails

Tools: trowel

Assembly: Plastering is far easier when you work with your separate MDF wainscot. This technique adds a

versatile Mediterranean ambiance without the chore of plastering a whole wall. Since it is wainscot and is meant to stand out, using tints is better than straight white. Have your paint store tint a batch of amber and a batch of sienna plaster. Apply a relatively thick amber coat to the MDF first with a trowel. Be sure each coat dries fully before applying the next. Apply another coat of amber, then follow that with a coat or more of sienna. Be a bit more sparing and chaotic with the sienna coat to achieve a timeworn look. Find some knotty pine chair rail (the cheapest pine) and stain it with either dark stain or coffee. Nail the pine in place above the hung, plastered MDF. Large-head iron nails will add greater Old World detail.

Chic Wallpaper Wainscot

Materials: paint, wallpaper, wallpaper paste, plain MDF chair rail

Tools: drop cloths, paint brush, paste brush

Assembly: Wallpaper your MDF wainscot or lower wall for a cheap and easy dose of major style. Find the style of paper that fits your design style, and feel free to find something bold. Use a standard wallpaper application process (wrap the paper around the edges of the MDF if you're using that). Use a plain beveled MDF chair rail and paint it to complement the wallpaper. Be sure to cover the top edge of wallpaper when you hang the rail.

Mexican Metalwork Masterpiece

Materials: paint, scrap metal, pine chair rail, and stain of your choice or tile, mortar, and a trowel

Tools: drop cloths, paint brushes or trowel

Assembly: Find decorative wrought iron, copper, or tin wall hangings. Cheaper yet, find flat metal pieces or old gates and fencing at a salvage shop. You'll be surprised at how cheap and folksy this look can be. Paint the wainscot board or lower wall a warm, dark color and mount the decorative metal pieces consistently across the wall. Sections of fence can be easily tacked to the MDF with U-tacks. As a chair rail for this style, stick with a stained pine or a row of Mexican tile.

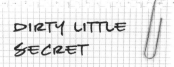
Country Eco-Chic

Materials: old barn slats (extra style points if there is chipped paint still on them)

Assembly: Try planking the slats side by side, and don't worry if they aren't totally flush. Just be sure to cut them all to the same length vertically. Get creative by mounting the fencing at a forty-five degree angle instead of simply vertical—this will achieve a rustic herringbone effect. Be sure to cut (and sand smooth) the top and bottom at the same angle you mount the fence at to keep the ends horizontally straight. No chair rail necessary here, though I like to use horizontal slats to give it a clean, capped-off look.

WORK WITH THE FIFTH WALL

Almost all rooms actually have *five* walls, but rarely does anyone pay attention to the last one. If you're seeking inspiration and a way to really instill some originality in your design, look up. The ceiling, left white in almost every room in every house in the country, is a blank canvas waiting for you to pay it some attention.

One of the ideas behind keeping the ceiling white is that it makes a room seem as big as possible. This is simply untrue. Now that you've added color and texture to your walls (and you have added some drama to the design of your walls, right?) a white ceiling is going to contrast starkly with the lower walls. Contrast generally has the effect of calling attention to something, and in this case it calls attention to the ceiling acting as a cap on the space. Especially if your room is small or short already, you'll want to decrease the contrast between the ceiling and the lower walls. If your walls have color, this means it's time to color the ceiling, too. Begin by considering a light tone shift from walls to ceiling—paint the ceiling two shades lighter than the color on the walls. This is the surest way to soften contrast and trick the eye into perceiving the room as taller than it is.

The ceiling can be more than a way to make the room appear larger. Because it is so architecturally separate from every other feature of a room, you can add tweaks of style that you might not add to a lower wall. That's one reason the ceilings of churches were so often given as canvases to the great Renaissance masters. Like Michelangelo, you can go beyond paint and use texturing and architectural features to create your own masterpiece. (Now I don't want to discourage your inner genius, but honestly I'd advise you to try a conservative stenciling before attempting your own *Creation of Adam*.)

Here are the best and most budget-friendly ways to enhance your fifth wall:

Paint

In addition to painting the ceiling lighter by two tones to make the room seem as large as possible, you can use paint to complement the room in more dramatic ways. Try using a color wheel to find a different but complementary color and see how radiant your room can be! Or focus your paint in one small area and try a stenciling that picks up on the theme of the room in whatever color you choose (start small, with nothing that will cover more than 20 percent of the total ceiling space—consider painting the borders of the ceiling to emphasize a large room's perimeter). Make sure the area you paint has either architectural lines (like a coved ceiling) or stenciled lines bordering it so as not to look sloppy. Picking up on ambient colors from the room's décor, from the central area rug for instance, will add to the fullness of your design's ambiance.

Wallpaper

The name implies otherwise, but there *are* many types of wallpaper that are meant for ceilings. Choose either a pattern that will enhance the overall décor (something that belongs to your intended design style) or opt for a textured wallpaper to add visual appeal. My favorite ceiling wallpapers replicate the texture and coloration of tin. You can even paint these wallpapers to customize what type of metal you want to imitate! You can go for either 100 percent coverage with textured wallpaper or just paper a portion of the ceiling. If you only cover a portion, you can highlight a focal area, sitting area, or other place you want to direct guests toward by papering above it. You'll want the wallpapered area of your ceiling delineated by architectural lines such as pitch changes in the ceiling, beams, or the inner areas of track lighting grids.

TEXTURED PATTERN

The stucco popcorn look is not as popular as it once was. Because it had such popularity for so long, stucco popcorn no longer has much style. My favorite faux-finishing techniques for the fifth wall are stenciling, metallics, wood texturing, and color washes. See the DIY Index, page 201.

ONE OF MY FAVE
BUDGET SAVERS—OPT
FOR "FAUX TIN CEILING
WALLPAPER" INSTEAD OF
THE REAL THING

PAINTING AND INSTALLING A CEILING MEDALLION

MATERIALS: ceiling medallion, paint

TOOLS: adhesive caulk, caulk gun

ASSEMBLY:

1. Paint and let your medallion dry before doing anything else.
2. Hold the medallion for someone to see before hanging, like you would when hanging a picture frame.
3. Apply a good amount of caulk to the flat, unornamented side of the medallion and press it firmly to the wall or ceiling. Hold for a minute or until the medallion sticks.

Medallions

Once made from heavy cast plaster, you can now purchase polyurethane foam medallions for a fraction of what medallions have cost for ages. Medallions add an elegant look even if painted the exact color of the ceiling. Better (and bolder) still, paint a medallion the color of other architectural features or of the lower walls. Also remember that a metallic paint or finish on a medallion can go as well with a modern look as with any of the traditional design styles.

Pressed Metal Panels and Faux Beams

Hugely popular in the Victorian era, pressed metal is a fantastic element that will entirely transform a boring space. As with imitation tin wallpaper, you can cover a portion of your ceiling instead of the whole thing. Even cheaper and easier (because of lighter hanging weight) are plastic panels. Plastics can also be used with faux finishes to create faux beams that will add a timeworn, rustic look to even the most urban spaces.

DIY
FAUX BEAMS

MATERIALS: four (or as many beams as you would like) 2x4s (cut to length of ceiling wall-to-wall length), three 1x4 pine planks cut to same length of your 2x4s, paint or wood stain (color of choice)

TOOLS: drill, wood screws, wood glue, paintbrush, stud finder, finishing nails, hammer (or nail gun)

ASSEMBLY: (friend or partner needed for this project)
1. Using the stud finder, find studs in your ceiling and mark these with light pencil.
2. Screw 2x4s into the ceiling approximately every 2 feet apart (spacing varies based on the size of the room).
3. Measure your 1x4 pine planks to fit around the 2x4 bracket in the ceiling.
4. Paint or stain the pine planks and let dry.
5. Using wood glue and nails, attach the two side pieces and the bottom of the 1x4 pine planks, creating a U-shaped beam.
6. Secure the hollow U-shaped planks with glue and nails to the 2x4s on the ceiling.

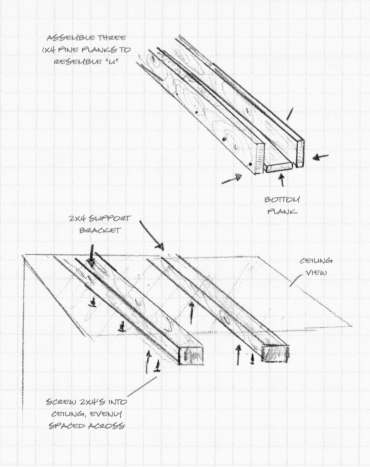

ASSEMBLE THREE 1X4 PINE PLANKS TO RESEMBLE "U"

BOTTOM PLANK

2X4 SUPPORT BRACKET

CEILING VIEW

SCREW 2X4'S INTO CEILING, EVENLY SPACED ACROSS

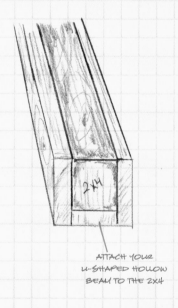

2X4

ATTACH YOUR U-SHAPED HOLLOW BEAM TO THE 2X4

GO GET 'EM!

I hope you're now excited to bring some color and style to the five walls of your room. Even if you only choose one of the several techniques I've told you about, you're already taking an important step away from white walls! You cannot underestimate the effect walls have on the feel of everything in a space, but you can use their effect to your advantage in a huge way.

PUTTING IT ALL TOGETHER
cohesion

Now you have a mission: Leave the white walls behind! You can paint them fully or just paint the architectural features. You can paint both the architectural features and all the walls in similar or in totally different colors to bring in a big dose of style. You can paint one wall a different color to make it a focal point, or go bold and use several different wall colors. Use faux finishes and the other budget-saving techniques that I've told you about (like wainscoting) to create architectural flair where there was only blank space before. Embrace the wonderful world of wallpaper and think of all the different ways you can apply it. Finally, don't forget the fifth wall—the ceiling—in all your consideration of how to change your room into the best environment for style by changing your walls.

LAYERING MULTIPLE COLORS OF
PLASTER CAN HAVE A LARGE
IMPACT ON A FOCAL WALL LIKE THIS *

CHAPTER FOUR

GOING GREEN FOR LESS

A List of Green Options Without Those that Wallop Your Wallet

It's common knowledge that we, as consumers, need to pay attention to the environmental impact we have. Homes and home goods have been at the forefront of the green movement for two big reasons. For most of us, it's our homes that consume the most energy of anything else we own, so there is a lot of room to trim our expenditure. Also, from basic building materials to high-tech goodies, everything a home needs can be provided for in a huge variety of ways. Finding which way is best is the soul of good design. You can see why designers of home goods love putting their minds to work to produce greener and greener goods. All of their effort has paid off with a huge range of new green products and procedures.

For me, preventing waste has always been part of good design. I love having a story for the items I design with, so I jump at the opportunity to save something from the dumpster, redesign its look or purpose, and recycle it for use in my rooms. It's amazing how much saved material and money a habit of preventing waste can bring.

There is a small problem when you're decorating on a tight budget, however, and that is the high price tag that comes with many of the newest green home products. There are many times when it's hard to even find a price until a company has walked you through all of the amazing innovations behind their product. Then you find out it's two grand for a new radiator, and you think maybe being an environmental crusader isn't yet for you.

If you're careful, though, and do your research (or use my own), you can find some incredible deals. I find lots of green and money-saving possibilities exist in homes already—there are ways to cheaply improve efficiency with some basic materials and your own two hands. Trust me, seeing the savings on an energy bill caused by your own smart efforts will cause an instant grin that won't go away for hours. There are also several ways to update in-home items to run in a cleaner, greener way—this saves you cash via the energy meter. Finally, there are a few big paydays to be had by purchasing green products and having a green auditor come over, assess your home, and cut you a sizeable check for your efforts.

There is green money to be pocketed by playing the green game.

TRUE CONFESSIONS

Most people become hesitant upon seeing the price tag of green items. Occasionally on *Design on a Dime* we are faced with decisions because of a new green option: Go green for more or save part of that precious $1,000 to add more to a room? It's a tough call; we often run the dilemma through the staff to get feedback. One hundred percent of the time, the vote favors saving money and putting more into décor so that the guests are that much more pleased with the transformation. When I've told guests about our dilemma after it's all done, they tend to give a sigh of relief—as if we'd made the tough call for them.

Extreme greenies might be upset at my confession. The truth, however, is that it would be dishonest to favor more expensive options for any reason when your show is supposed to be dedicated to decorating on a tight budget. As a big supporter of the green movement, however, I always try to locate products that can be *both* the green option *and* the cheap option. Fortunately, because saving waste also means saving money, green and cheap overlap *a lot*.

SUSTAINABLE BAMBOO
WINE BOTTLE HOLDER

MY THREE Rs

During my career of designing for less than a thousand dollars, I found a system that made everything easier and quicker and that saves me some dough on my makeovers. It's all about the three Rs: *Recycle*, *Refurbish*, *Repurpose*.

Recycle

Save the earth and some money by turning old objects into new décor. Do it yourself (DIY) enthusiasts often recycle old items into new items. I believe creativity is part of almost everyone's nature. I encourage you to think outside the box, follow your instincts, and look at objects from a variety of angles. You never know when a décor idea is going to pop in your head. Flea market finds and unused items around the house can provide an endless source of DIY materials.

DIY recycling can bring your creative side to life. Get together with friends and swap unused and unwanted items. Have a "recycle party" where you turn old items into useful and decorative ones. Make recycling a habit.

Refurbish

My motto has always been, "waste equals bad taste." In this case, throwing out perfectly good furniture and decorative items without at least giving it a second chance is such a waste of reusable resources. New accents and faux finishes really come to bear when refurbishing an old piece.

WHAT "GREEN" MEANS

Products and materials can be considered green for many reasons. The raw materials used in making them may come from sources considered environmentally friendly, such as wood from certified forests, recycled materials, and rapidly renewable agricultural fibers. Some products are considered green because they are manufactured in a way that releases minimal pollutants or avoids toxic byproducts. Other products are green because they minimize the negative effects of construction, such as avoiding the need to excavate a foundation or because they help a building minimize its use of energy or water. Products also can be green because they do not introduce pollutants into the home environment, or because they help remove pollutants.

A REPURPOSED ANTIQUE BABY CRIB NOW SERVES AS COOL STORAGE FOR BLANKETS

Repurpose

Is it unreasonable to think if you purchased something—whether an old bookshelf, a plastic hamper, or a set of dining room chairs—that it couldn't later serve you a different, maybe a more useful purpose? Repurposing everyday household items is one of the easiest ways to reduce your carbon footprint and save some precious dollars on your next makeover. It's really quite fun and challenging to come up with new ways to use old things. Sometimes it's just a matter of turning something on its side.

NEW GREEN OPPORTUNITY

Increased awareness about environmental issues has yielded new opportunities for those of us who go green. To my longstanding three Rs, I'll add a fourth: *Reward*, or strategies for saving money—and sometimes even earning money!—by being eco-efficient.

The list below is the result of my research and practice; these ideas bring style and savings while decreasing your environmental impact and the energy it takes to run your home. *Recycle, Refurbish,* and *Repurpose* items like crazy to save lots of money. I've also included ways to *Reward* yourself—to save or receive enough money by going green to make the purchase worth it financially.

THE GREAT GREEN LIST

Recycle

New old material: Look for dry, fallen wood in nature or seek out scrap yards and barnyard companies to find a wealth of extremely cheap woods and metals with tons of character. Not a lot of work is required for many DIY projects with old wood because you want the natural look to come through. For example:

Homasote® Burlap Panels: Adorn your windows with simple, natural elegance. Composed of an all-natural, heavyweight jute fabric laminated to fiberboard, these decorative, tack-able shades are ideal for a range of applications from family rooms to children's bedrooms. They can be used as a finished paneling in their natural state or painted to adapt to any color or décor. Check out EarthShade.com for a huge catalog. I love using jute and burlap with Asian, Contemporary, Shabby Chic, and Eclectic style spaces.

IceStone: IceStone is an ideal green countertop material made from 100 percent recycled glass mixed with cement. These gorgeous countertops are highly durable and beautiful and fit all design styles because it is totally customizable in color and finishing. Floors and wall coverings are also available. Check out IceStone.biz to browse. This is the sort of element that adds character and a story to your space.

Tame your towels: Save terrycloth towels from the trash by using them as lining for a pet's bed, handy rags, or sewing swatches into an eclectic throw blanket.

Recycle your trash!: This is a big one. You can save 2,400 pounds of carbon dioxide a year by recycling half of the waste your household generates. If everyone recycled, many goods would become cheaper to produce. Earth 911 is a company that can help you find recycling resources in your area. It's good to start the habit, too, because many reforms are being enacted across the country to penalize non-recyclers. Good thing you're not one! If you have a recycling receptacle inside, embrace the style: Antique tin or copper containers will contain the mess and look better than the usual plastic trash can. Stowing a receptacle out of plain sight—under the sink or in the garage—is, of course, a great option.

Refurbish

Repaint: Sometimes a fresh coat of paint is all you need. There's no need to stop at a mere color change, either. Try stencils or other great faux-finishing techniques. Browse my favorite faux finishes on pages 12–14 before you throw any substantial item out!

Workplace throwaways: Ugly workplace items like drawers from filing cabinets are thrown out all the time because no one wants to bring them home. Uncanny colors and metallic paint, though, can turn formerly ugly metal bins into stylish (and handy!) containers to have around the house.

Pig in a blanket: Save 1,000 pounds of carbon dioxide a year by wrapping your water heater in an insulated, fireproof blanket. Simply secure the blanket in the back of the heater with staples or duct tape. Save an average of 550 pounds of carbon dioxide per year by setting the water heater to no higher than 120 degrees Fahrenheit. Designing and building your very own radiator cover is an easy and highly rewarding DIY project. If you're looking for a starter project, this is it. Refer to page 105, for step-by-step instructions.

Insulate: Properly insulating your walls and ceilings can save 25 percent of your home heating bill and 2,000 pounds of carbon dioxide a year. Caulking and weather-stripping can save another 1,700 pounds per year. The Consumer Federation of America has more information on how to find consultants who will walk you through all the prices and steps to improving home insulation. This is one of those things where with a phone call and some money spent on an appointment you can save tens of thousands of dollars in the long run. Simply ask the consultant for a savings estimate . . . then treat yourself to a little something when you find out how much cash will be staying in your pocket in the future.

Lighting update: Eleek is a lighting restoration service that speaks to the important concept of updating existing goods. Keep your beautiful old lamps

THE EASIEST WAY TO START BEING GREEN IS TO SWITCH YOUR LIGHT BULBS TO CFLs AND LEDS *

...ays, CFLs emit a warm, inviting light that can replace incandescent bulbs in pretty much every location. And they are more energy efficient, using up to 75% less energy and lasting up to 10 times longer than incandescents. Avoid using with a dimmer or multiple power switch as this will reduce the life of the bulb. CFLs contain a tiny amount of mercury, so please take advantage of local recycling options for disposal.

The new genera-tion LEDs are only slightly less bright than incandescents and can now replace most stan-dard bulbs. They last an amazing 60,000 hours or more and expend minimum energy. Since the power intake of an LED bulb is so low, special LED fixtures and dimmer switches must be used with them.

500 LOCAL

CFL COMPACT...

LED LIGHT-EMITTING DIODE

and make them cheaper to turn on. When Eleek restores a light fixture, every piece of a fixture is taken apart, repaired, and restored to its original splendor. Its wiring is updated to comply with modern codes and standards, and a new lamp base is installed so it works with energy-efficient bulbs such as CFLs and LEDs. This will score you points with any energy auditor you invite over. Check out Eleekinc.com. Reviving antique lighting with Eleek will make you want to spend days browsing flea markets and antique stores for cool lighting elements.

Repurpose

Keep molding handy: Old molding, after some fresh paint, can bring a facelift to almost any wood furniture. I rarely throw molding out, especially when it has cool beveling. It's not hard to store a box of it in the garage or basement.

You've got mail: Always think about what an item can do if it's moved away from its initial function. One of my favorite tips is to never throw away wood shutters: Simply leaning them against a wall provides a great series of slots to sort your family's mail.

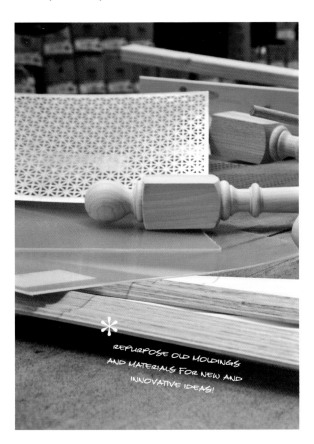

REPURPOSE OLD MOLDINGS AND MATERIALS FOR NEW AND INNOVATIVE IDEAS!

Reward

Chill out: Almost half of the energy we use in our homes goes to heating and cooling. Move your thermostat down 2 degrees Fahrenheit in winter and up 2 degrees Fahrenheit in summer to save about 2,000 pounds of carbon dioxide a year! This sort of change can easily be accommodated with your at-home wardrobe. Show off those arms in a tank top in the summer—also, going barefoot when indoors will cool you down and keep the house cleaner. In winter, this small change is the difference between wearing a sweater instead of just a T-shirt. Come on. Wearing only a tee in winter is just unnatural!

EcoSmart™ Fires: These products are design magic, especially in urban apartments where fireplaces are rarely available. They are environmentally friendly open fireplaces, installable in walls, outdoors, or freestanding indoors. They are fueled by easily renewable denatured ethanol, which burns clean into steam, heat, and a miniscule amount of carbon dioxide. These fireplaces are virtually maintenance free. They are flue-less and require neither installation nor utility connection. Tax credits up to $1,500 are available in the United States. My favorite is the EcoSmart Zeta, so named because of its elliptical shape that pays homage to its Greek origins. Ecosmartfire.com shows off the breathtaking selection of designs.

Use sustainable wood: Foundation Bamboo makes an exotic and beautiful range of flooring derived from one of the most sustainable woods there is. Bamboo forests grow back a lot faster than traditional hardwoods. Solid-strip bamboo flooring takes long narrow strips of bamboo and laminates them together. Choose between horizontal grain—wider strips that display the knuckles of the bamboo—or vertical grain—narrower strips. Both horizontal and vertical grains are available in "carbonized" (heat-treated for a warm amber color) and "natural" (bathed in non-toxic peroxide for a blond color). Bamboo's rapid growth doesn't just make it sustainable—it makes it cheaper than other woods you might use for a floor because the manufacturing and harvesting methods are evolving at a great rate.

Solid-strip flooring comes in elegant 6-foot planks and an oversized $3^{4/5}$-inch width. They are precision milled with a tongue and groove on all four sides and a modern looking micro-bevel. Each board is then coated with a sealer coat on all exposed surfaces (for improved moisture protection) and seven layers of water-based, UV-cured, aluminum oxide modified polyurethane. Bamboo flooring is suitable for residential or commercial applications. It can contribute LEED points to your project in the areas of Materials & Resources (rapidly renewable resource), and Indoor Environmental Quality (a low-emitting product). Make re-flooring cheaper and greener when it has to be done.

This style can enhance an Asian element in a space, but is not limited to that design style alone. Bamboo naturally looks like a light wood, but plenty of stained options are available.

Another option for replacing long growth, expensive woods is eucalyptus. "Lyptus" is the trade name for ecologically responsibly harvested eucalyptus, which comes in a huge range of light and dark woods. Like bamboo, eucalyptus grows at a much quicker rate than other woods and is harvested from groves in Brazil and Australia dedicated to preventing deforestation.

Non-toxic everything: Thinking about a DIY project that requires paint, finish, or adhesive? Every hardware store should carry non-toxic versions of each, which will not only release far less pollutants into the air than standard versions but will make the work much easier on your eyes, nose, and skin. Seek paints and stains with a low-V.O.C. label. It essentially means that less nasty things are released by the paint. Also try my personal recipe for wood staining with coffee grounds (see page 11).

Light it up: Replace regular incandescent light bulbs with a compact fluorescent lights (CFL), which use 60 percent less energy than regular bulbs. This simple switch will save about 300 pounds of carbon dioxide a year. If every family in the United States made the switch, we'd reduce carbon dioxide by more than 90 billion pounds! You can purchase CFLs in bulk online from the Energy Federation. The difference is you need to wait a few moments before the bulb is glowing at full strength, but even within the first second you can read a magazine without straining your eyes. Also, enjoy rarely breaking the step ladder out for replacing these long-lasting bulbs. How much motivation do you need to screw in a light bulb?

Be the taxman: Save up to 30 percent on your energy bill and 1,000 pounds of carbon dioxide a year by getting a home energy audit. Most municipal utility companies offer free home energy audits to find where your home is poorly insulated or energy inefficient. Energy Star can help you find an energy specialist if your energy provider cannot. Auditors will tell you about government tax incentives as well. Imagine a world where you're actually happy to see a taxman knocking at your door—I know, it's a little hard for me, too . . . but he cut me a check last time he came!

Pimp out your . . . air filters: Save 350 pounds of carbon dioxide a year by cleaning or replacing dirty air filters on your furnace and air conditioner every month. Keeping tabs on your filters makes your heating and cooling systems much more energy efficient. Most people use cheap blue air filters; these should be replaced every thirty days. But if you really want to go green, you should spend around $15 for permanent air filters—all you need to do is spray them down with a hose every month. These will save you money on filters in the long run and trap more dust and general ickiness—keeping your air cleaner and your heating and cooling systems at top efficiency. Make sure you buy a model that fits your brand of furnace and air conditioner.

Be a star: Look for the Energy Star label on new appliances when making new purchases. If each household in the United States replaced its existing appliances with the most efficient models available, we would eliminate 175 million tons of carbon dioxide emissions every year! Energy Star appliances have been around for years, so buying used is no problem. Also, you can aspire to have that classy little star emblem on every appliance. Talk about design cohesion!

Hang it up: Use a clothesline instead of a dryer whenever possible. You can save 700 pounds of carbon dioxide when you air-dry your clothes for 6 months out of the year. Dryers are among the most expensive appliances to run in the home, so make summer your cheapest season on the energy meter. Instead of buying dryer sheets with scents like "fresh air" and "sunshine," you can use the real stuff!

Tune out: Simply turning off your television, DVD player, stereo, and computer when you're not using them will save thousands of pounds of carbon dioxide a year. Too often we leave these items in "sleep" mode for hours, when in seconds we can turn them off and back on when

*HOW ABOUT THIS FULLY
SUSTAINABLE KITCHEN—
EVEN THE TEAPOT IS
GREEN!

we need them. Also unplug chargers like those for laptop computers—even if they are not plugged into the computer, they still burn energy. Every time you tug the plug out of the wall you're doing your part to save the world.

Dish the dirt: Save 100 pounds of carbon dioxide per year by running your dishwasher on the energy-saving setting, and only when there's a full load. This will also save you time spent unloading and reloading. Honing your skills at the modern art that is properly stacking dishes in a dishwasher will lead to annual energy savings. Think of arranging plates, bowls, cups, and mugs to be the most space efficient as practice in the art of good design.

Can you dig it: Plant a tree! If this sounds cliché, just look at the numbers. A single tree will absorb one ton of carbon dioxide over its lifetime. Shade provided by trees over your house can also reduce your air-conditioning bill by 10 to 15 percent. The Arbor Day Foundation has tons of information on planting and provides free trees for planting to members. For almost no effort, you can provide a real estate value boost for future generations who live in your home. Wait for a nice day and have a good time with it!

Green power: In many areas, you can switch to energy generated by clean, renewable sources such as the wind and sun without having equipment installed in your home. The Green Power Network is a good place to start to figure out what's available in your area. If you do decide to spring for solar power at your home, you can make money from it by selling excess energy back to the utility company. It's like setting up an easy small business with almost no management.

Walk it out: Drive less and walk, bike, carpool, or take mass transit more! You'll save 1 pound of carbon dioxide for every mile you don't drive. The potential to lose weight, lower stress, and save money is huge! A leisurely bike ride in the spring or summer can hardly be beat, and buying baskets can allow you to run errands while exercising and saving money.

PUTTING IT ALL TOGETHER
cohesion

Bringing several green design solutions together into your home does more than enhance the cohesion of your space. It even does more than save the world. If you utilize the advice in this list, it will save you money!

RECYCLED GLASS COUNTER TOPS LOOK HIP AND MODERN

PART TWO

TRANSFORMING YOUR HOME

A Room-by-Room Guide

to Infusing Your Home with Style

CHAPTER FIVE

ENTRYWAYS

Making a Perfect First Impression

Everyone knows the expression "don't judge a book by its cover," which I agree with. (Hey, look at my book—awesome cover, awesome book; there's the answer to that old dilemma!). I think you can treat the entryway like the cover of the interior design of your home. An entryway is the beginning of the story of your home—which really means it is the first impression people see of your story. If it seems like the stakes are raised . . . it's because they are—we ain't decorating no mudroom!

But so many people are content to leave their entryways as empty space with some shoes lined up by the wall. (Worse with the shoes strewn all over!) Others simply hang whatever extra items they have up on the walls and head back to the main home thinking they're done decorating. This is the wrong way to go about it! You need to give a personal treatment to most everything in an entryway. Incorporate organization and a lack of obstruction into your plan, but find clever ways to show people who you are. You can think of your entryway as a mini-museum of the lives of you and your family.

A few other problems that prevent people from designing their entryways with style and flair are typically the cost, existing architectural obstructions, and lack of a formal entry "room." Let's face it, this is not a high-priority place to redecorate, so many people would rather save decorating money for other spaces. Well, I'll help you drop that idea in no time. The entryway is the perfect spot for you to begin your decorating adventure! From DIY projects that embrace your personality to simple solutions that make you look like a decorating guru, I'll cover some of my favorite and fun methods to design to *your* style. Better still, the best DIY projects for the entryway will use items you already own (collections, heirlooms, and other souvenirs of your life) to bring most of their style so you don't need to spend much on fancy materials.

DON'TS AND DOS

Don't:

* Clutter your entryway with bulky objects like dressers, hutches, etc.
* Clutter your entryway with too many loose, small odds and ends.
* Place items that can be easily knocked over on shelves without protection.
* Use organizing feature like hat racks, umbrella bins, jacket trees, show cubbies, etc., that don't get use, add to style, or could be substituted for smaller options.
* Stop thinking of how you can personalize *your* entryway to set the stage for the rest of the home.

Q.D.E. ALERT
function

Your entryway has kind of a tricky function: You want to allow people to pass directly through, maybe take off their shoes and jackets, but you also want to tempt them to pause for a moment and consider the space. This can be tough to balance! An equal mixture of organization and style is required.

I find that bold décor, compelling wall-hung photography, and an inexpensive, narrow tall vase filled with a few regional branches are excellent ways express style in an entryway. If possible, try relating the furnishings to hobbies, places you've been, and other favorite things. The best goal to have in mind is for your design to cause a guest to walk into your main space after walking through the decorated entryway and comment to you about something interesting they saw as they entered. This not only tells strangers and new friends something about you they probably don't know but will stick in people's memories when they fondly recall your home.

Do:

* Focus on convenience for your guests and provide for it in the right details.
* Incorporate easy to spot, condensed or multi-functional organizing spaces for items like shoes, coats, hats, etc. (There are plenty of DIY suggestions further in.)
* Use décor and comforting flourishes to tempt guests to linger in the entryway.
* Find lighting that complements your space and design style.

TRUE CONFESSIONS

On *Design on a Dime* and *Takeover My Makeover*, we are rarely asked to touch the entryway—if someone is given the choice between redecorating a living room or entryway, how often would they say: "Oh, my entryway! Redo my entryway!"? It doesn't happen.

But I walk onto a job every day through the entryway, so if it rubs me wrong, it's in my nature to stop and inspect the issue. Plus, I can't let a poorly decorated entry ruin the buildup to one of my masterful makeovers! Usually I don't have the time or budget to put much energy into redecorating this little space, but I still offer redecorating tips and little DIY ideas to the guests off camera. Owners' reactions are never mild. Some people grab a pen

Q.D.E. ALERT
ambiance

The entry is the very first opportunity to make a statement about your home and yourself. In this space you can add strong, unique ambiance—but you cannot throw stuff into people's way to do so! If the path through the entry is cluttered or overly indirect, the whole presentation will be ruined. Use color and lighting levels to create ambiance for your décor to show in, but don't position anything to be in people's way. Ambiance in entryways is a great example of sprezzatura; use subtle design tricks to display your design, but let your layout show that you're not fazed if anyone just passes right on through. (Don't worry, if you take my advice, they won't.)

and paper, start writing it down, and thank me like crazy. Other people become quite touchy! Like I insulted them; like I said, "Listen, the living room is going well, but we need to talk about the way you dress." I always feel awful afterward (or I make it look like I do), and, until I figured out why this happened, I was surprised.

After three blowups I realized what the problem was. People do recognize, maybe not even consciously, that their entryway is a reflection of themselves, so they take it personally. Small wonder, then, that they react so strongly to my advice about changing things! But I swear, the entryway affects guests' impression of the whole rest of the house. Even the initial smell of a house affects a person's perception of how you keep your home.

A COMMON PROBLEM: CLUTTER

Hats hung wherever possible, coats draped all over, and shoes everywhere! This is not just a cluttered entryway—it's my recurring nightmare! Clutter from guests, family, and life in general is a big problem in entryways, where an unimpeded flow of energy is top priority. You need to prepare to support about double the number of people in your family if you want to avoid stacking coats elsewhere all the time. The number one thing to pay attention to is shoe storage. Shoes and boots cannot be hung and take up lots of floor space. You need some sort of organizing solution. Here's what to do with . . .

The Shoes

Wait! Please, I beg you, please don't go out and buy a wire shoe rack and stick it in your hallway by the door. Look for a sturdy wood option that complements your design. Wood is also great for making your own shoe storage, because it is the easiest material with which to build any storage system. I like using conversions of large furniture to build a multipurpose storage place for shoes and a spot to sit when putting them back on.

DIY
BOOKSHELF CONVERSION TO ENTRY STORAGE

MATERIALS: 3¾" MDF squares, old three-tier bookshelf (find at local thrift store or in your own home), industrial casters (wheels), latex paint to match existing bookshelf (or paint entire piece the color of choice), cheap wall mirror, four individual coat hooks

TOOLS: wood glue, wood screws, drill, industrial strength adhesive, clamps, circular saw, measuring tape

ASSEMBLY:

1. Measure and cut MDF squares to fit as dividers in the bottom two shelves in the unit.
2. Secure dividers with wood glue and wood screws.
3. Install industrial casters (wheels) with the drill and screws to the bottom of the bookshelf to allow for mobility if needed.
4. Paint everything one color if desired.
5. Using industrial-strength glue and clamps, adhere the wall mirror to the side of bookshelf (for vanity reasons . . . need to be sure you look one last time before you head out the door).
6. Drill your four coat hooks on the opposite side of the bookshelf.

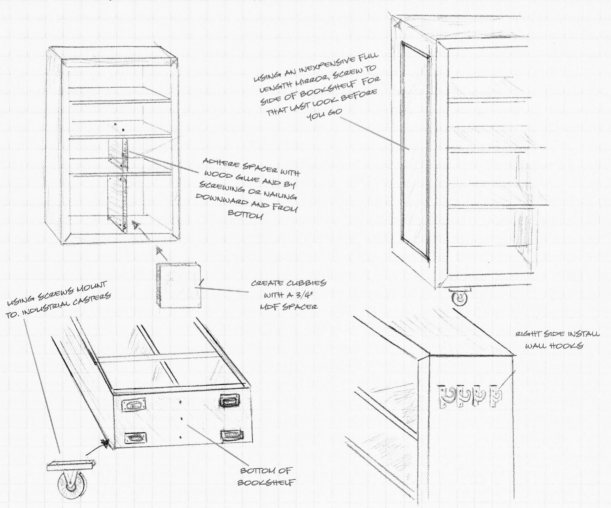

USING AN INEXPENSIVE FULL LENGTH MIRROR, SCREW TO SIDE OF BOOKSHELF FOR THAT LAST LOOK BEFORE YOU GO

ADHERE SPACER WITH WOOD GLUE AND BY SCREWING OR NAILING DOWNWARD AND FROM BOTTOM

CREATE CUBBIES WITH A 3/4" MDF SPACER

USING SCREWS MOUNT TO. INDUSTRIAL CASTERS

RIGHT SIDE INSTALL WALL HOOKS

BOTTOM OF BOOKSHELF

DIY
PICKET FENCE STORAGE BENCH

MATERIALS: decorative trim molding, old chest, decorative corner appliqué, wood fence post toppers, 3" foam, cotton batting, fabric of choice, ½" MDF board, 2' long 2x4 strip, latex paint of choice, 4' by 4' white picket fence (or paint it white yourself)

TOOLS: industrial-strength glue, nail gun (or hammer and finishing nails), drill, screws, handsaw, jigsaw

ASSEMBLY:

1. Start by adhering decorative molding on front, side, and top of chest with glue.
2. Glue on corner appliqués.
3. Screw fence post tops to the bottom of the chest to use as decorative legs for chest (paint legs color of choice).
4. Upholster MDF bench top with foam, batting, and fabric.
5. Screw a 2x4 strip on the inside back wall of the chest.
6. Attach the picket fence to the back of the chest; be sure to screw into the 2x4 for maximum support.
7. Paint the entire piece desired color.

TOP CUSHION MADE FROM FOAM BATTING AND FABRIC ON AN MDF BOARD GETS SCREWED TO TOP LID OF CHEST

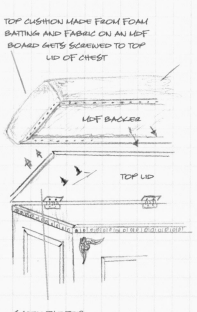

MDF BACKER

TOP LID

SCREW THE TOP CUSHION THROUGH THE BOTTOM PORTION OF THE LID

USE RECLAIMED FENCE PIECE FROM SALVAGE SHOP

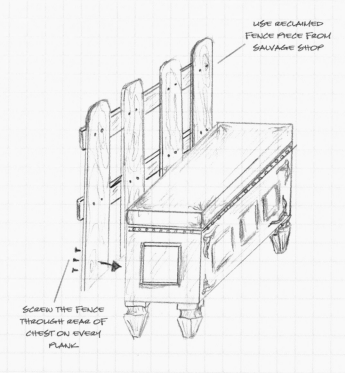

SCREW THE FENCE THROUGH REAR OF CHEST ON EVERY PLANK

The Coats

The next thing you're going to want to pay attention to is a coatrack. This can be a blast, because coatracks have been necessary forever and there are so many styles from so many different time periods. Finding an antique coatrack, cleaning it off, and placing it in your entryway as is yields gorgeous, time-tested style. Also, find an umbrella basket with a small spatial profile and a bold style profile.

The Hats

I like to let hats lend to my décor. The obvious, easy approach is just to purchase a few wall-mounted hooks (buy hooks in any hardware store in a variety of finishes for pocket change). Hang the hooks on one wall (typically the wall that sits behind the door as it opens to hide upon first

DIY
THE MULTIPLE FRAME COLLAGE

MATERIALS: pictures, hanging frames with flat edges (at least six), tacks

TOOLS: hammer, clamps, wood glue

ASSEMBLY:

1. Purchase frames in a variety that match your design style: varied size and look if you want an eclectic feel, or uniform size with slight color variation for more disciplined styles.
2. Arrange the frames so that their edges are flush, and adhere them together with wood glue. You can go beyond a normal square, but keep the general shape of the collage geometric so that the outside edges are mostly straight lines.
3. Hang the cluster on as many tacks as needed to support it. You'll need to use most of the hanging setups on the frames.

DIY
DOORKNOB COAT RACK

MATERIALS: one piece of approximately 3' x 5" reclaimed barn wood (or old board—the more layered paint and chips, the better), white paint, four or five reclaimed door knobs (all different finishes are fine—try to find old ones that are just for pulling; no hardware inside), wood screws

TOOLS: chain for roughing up wood, jigsaw, drill, screws, paintbrush, stud finder

ASSEMBLY:

1. Rough up your piece of barn wood (if it needs it) with a chain or baseball bat.
2. Jigsaw some jagged edges on each side of your barn wood.
3. Dry brush on some white paint if needed.
4. Screw the doorknobs onto the barn wood plank.
5. Using your stud finder, locate studs in the wall and mark them then screw the barn wood directly into studs (if you don't have studs then use wall anchors).

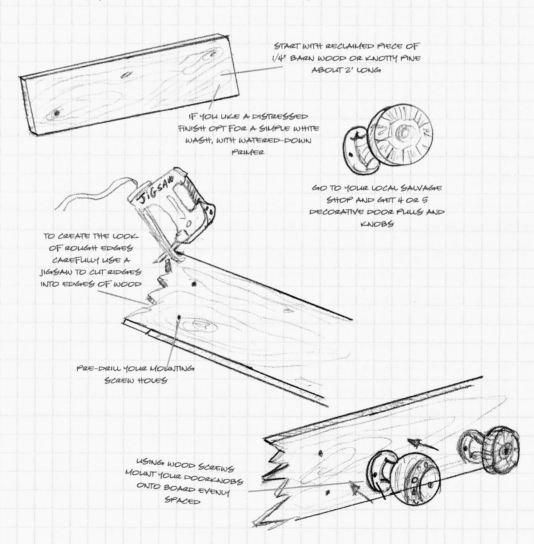

START WITH RECLAIMED PIECE OF 1/4" BARN WOOD OR KNOTTY PINE ABOUT 2' LONG

IF YOU LIKE A DISTRESSED FINISH OPT FOR A SIMPLE WHITE WASH, WITH WATERED-DOWN PRIMER

GO TO YOUR LOCAL SALVAGE SHOP AND GET 4 OR 5 DECORATIVE DOOR PULLS AND KNOBS

JIGSAW

TO CREATE THE LOOK OF ROUGH EDGES CAREFULLY USE A JIGSAW TO CUT RIDGES INTO EDGES OF WOOD

PRE-DRILL YOUR MOUNTING SCREW HOLES

USING WOOD SCREWS MOUNT YOUR DOORKNOBS ONTO BOARD EVENLY SPACED

DIY
THE STANDING DISPLAY TABLE

MATERIALS: old wooden end table, dark stain, velvet leather fabric

TOOLS: paintbrush, staple gun, ruler

ASSEMBLY:

1. Wash and stain the end table a dark color.
2. Measure the tabletop.
3. Purchase enough velvet fabric to cover the top of the table and wrap under the edges. Look for a color to match your décor.
4. Position the velvet on the tabletop so it is covered. Staple an edge of the velvet to the underside of the tabletop.
5. Staple an opposite edge of fabric under the tabletop from your first staple. Continue stapling from opposite ends until the velvet is taut.

DIRTY LITTLE SECRET

STAY FLEXIBLE

I love functional fixed objects. Floating shelves coming out of the wall, for instance, are a great space-and money-saving way to add style, display, and storage to a room. In the entryway, however, consider keeping fixed objects like this on the narrower side. Chances are high that you'll be carrying large things through the entryway. Even an armload of groceries can be annoying if your path is crowded by immovable objects (and it's a leading cause of bruised funny bones!). Even if you need someone to help you move it, make sure furniture in the entryway is movable for those times you'll need to haul things through. It's all about foresight.

entry. Space them with around 7 inches between them. Ideally you are safe to hang around four or five hooks in a row. I like to stagger them at slightly varying heights for a visual twist. But really, it's your call. You can repurpose anything, from garden hooks with age and character to odd industrial and architectural scraps—take this opportunity to infuse some personal style. Part of design is about expressing your personality and if you're known as the cool dude or chick who sports the funky hats, this is an especially good chance to tell something about the design style of your home or about yourself—you now have the perfect, prominent display spot. Just take care not to overdo it. Hats can add to a design style. Old Country-style woven reed hats or cotton bonnets hanging in the entry are perfect for a Country or Shabby Chic entry. A 1950s-style pinstriped fedora can add to a swanky pad's energy.

FRAMES FOR PERSONAL FLAIR

I want to help inspire you to use DIY projects to frame your personal items or demonstrate your artistic talent. As far as we're concerned, there are three sizes of décor for your entryway: small (fits on a desktop surface), medium (hangs on a wall), and large (placed on the floor, to the side).

ENTRYWAY LIGHTING

It's traditional for entryways to have a single, bright overhead light source that illuminates the whole space. If you live in an apartment complex, it's usually a generic, industrial fixture hung above the door as you enter . . . not the most attractive option. Here are some alternate options for an apartment or house that will enhance your personal décor to subtly bring more attention to your design.

Sconces

These are a great option if you have electrical sources already in place on the wall. If not, there's no need to start drilling through the wall. IKEA sells inexpensive wall-mounted sconces that you can plug into an outlet (cord covers can hide unsightly electrical dangles). Choosing a sconce that expresses your home's design style is important, so pay attention to shape, metal color, and design. The important question with sconces is, "in what direction is my light source going to be pointing?" If the sconce shoots up, it will cast more general light; if it shoots down or to the sides, more directed light.

Decent sconces range from $25 to $75.

Standing Floor and Task Lamps

Traditionally used in other parts of the home, these two options can be a nice accompaniment to an entry vignette. If you have a narrow console, a task light is classy and useful. If a single chair and umbrella caddy are paired in your entry, try a third element like a standing floor lamp to complete your grouping. Pay attention to lamp shade textures, colors, and transparency to pull together your cohesive design or theme.

Stylish floor and task lamps can be bought online for $15 to $50.

DIRTY LITTLE SECRET

MAKE AN "UNEXPECTED" UMBRELLA BASKET

I could tell you to build an umbrella basket from scratch, but between the need to make it watertight and the cost of the metal you're likely to buy and need to bend, it's not really worth it. Instead, find a decorative, plain metal or ceramic container that strikes your eye—just keep size in mind. (Tall and square floral vases, old metal wash bins, even small wine barrels can work well.) Once you find a gem, repurpose it as a place for umbrellas. If the finish isn't exactly what you like, but the size and shape are, then use faux finishing techniques like stencils, metallic finishes, and color washes (See page 52) to make it fit tightly (or clash brightly) with the theme of the other furnishings in the entryway.

DIY
THE FLOATING CATCH-ALL SHELF

MATERIALS: one 2x4 about 2' long for a wall cleat, four pieces of 1x4 knotty pine or MDF about 2½' long, paint or stain, wood glue

TOOLS: stud finder, pencil, drill, screws or nails, handsaw or chop saw, paintbrush

ASSEMBLY:

1. Using your stud finder, mark in pencil the areas where studs are in your wall.
2. Screw the 2x4 into the area of the wall you want to place your floating shelf/console.
3. Paint or stain facing pieces of 1x4 wood and let dry.
4. Assemble all four pieces around the 2x4 on the wall, cutting to fit, with wood glue, screws, and/or nails (fill nail holes with wood fill, sand, and paint after installation).

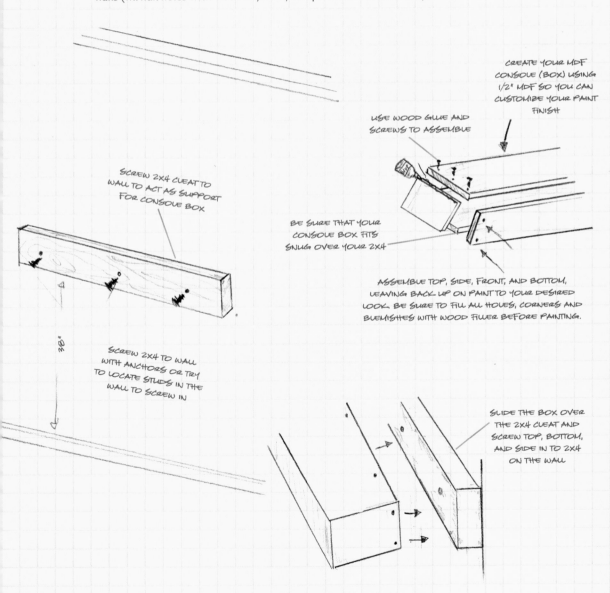

SCREW 2X4 CLEAT TO WALL TO ACT AS SUPPORT FOR CONSOLE BOX

SCREW 2X4 TO WALL WITH ANCHORS OR TRY TO LOCATE STUDS IN THE WALL TO SCREW IN

38"

CREATE YOUR MDF CONSOLE (BOX) USING 1/2" MDF SO YOU CAN CUSTOMIZE YOUR PAINT FINISH

USE WOOD GLUE AND SCREWS TO ASSEMBLE

BE SURE THAT YOUR CONSOLE BOX FITS SNUG OVER YOUR 2X4

ASSEMBLE TOP, SIDE, FRONT, AND BOTTOM, LEAVING BACK UP ON PAINT TO YOUR DESIRED LOOK. BE SURE TO FILL ALL HOLES, CORNERS AND BLEMISHES WITH WOOD FILLER BEFORE PAINTING.

SLIDE THE BOX OVER THE 2X4 CLEAT AND SCREW TOP, BOTTOM, AND SIDE IN TO 2X4 ON THE WALL

Chandeliers

The best way to bring instant drama to a hallway entry. I am a big fan of entry chandeliers, since they come in any design style and can occupy a central place in a design. Scale and size is really important when choosing a chandelier since it can easily overpower an entry if it is too big or too ornate. In my opinion, dimmers are a must if you're considering a chandelier.

Chandeliers cost $50 to $150, but they can add a center to your whole entryway.

Track Lighting

Cheap, easy, and highly functional, track lighting is a good option for entryways, especially if you have a hallway with art or shelves full of personalized display items. You can pin the spotlight on an object and give your entry a gallery feel. The beauty of track lighting is the ability to control the light heads to point in any direction and to control the amount of distinct sources you can have on the ceiling.

Track lighting costs $30 to $60 depending on length and number of lamps.

Attached Art Lighting

A more sleek, inexpensive way to illuminate your artwork in the entry is with clamp-on LED art lights (IKEA is one place that sells them). These fairly inexpensive light sources are specifically made for illuminating your artwork and can be clamped directly to a frame or attached to the wall. A series of these lights over your framed art can really bring a dramatic, evening lighting effect.

Attached art lighting can be picked up cheaply, between $20 and $40.

GO GET 'EM!

Now hopefully you're inspired not to abandon your entryway to being a bland mudroom and you'll instead embrace it as the perfect place to represent your story and that of your home. I hope you try some of these DIY projects as not just cheap and fun ways to create new items, but as ways to overcome DIY fear—if you don't have those fears then you must be a bold person, and that (or other traits!) will certainly show in your wonderful new entryway.

DIRTY LITTLE SECRET

EXIT COURTESY

There is one piece of furniture that I consider essential to an entryway—a chair. People need a place to sit down while they put their shoes back on! Other seating, like a bench or a window seat, is preferable, but if you're dealing with a small space then a chair is ten times as good as letting your guests hop around on one foot pulling on their shoes. Another great thing to keep in the entryway—a shoehorn. If guests have an easy place to tie their shoes before they leave, it will make their memory of your home that much better.

PUTTING IT ALL TOGETHER
cohesion

The entryway is a little space that can show tons of style! Pick and choose your lighting and color scheme (and fragrance) to complement all of your new displays and organizing handiwork. Collect small, medium, and large items that tell something about you and figure out what to group together in a display and what to let stand alone. Add conveniences for your guests that show them you care. Be sure guests can pass through with ease . . . unless, of course, they are caught up gazing at your warm, personal mini-museum!

CHAPTER SIX

LIVING SPACES

Designing the Heart of Your Home

The living room is where we designers like to shine. The living room offers the opportunity to be a bit more daring and experimental since the space's function is not so sharply defined as, say, your kitchen or bathroom. Let's face it. The room's title is pretty vague. It's the room for living, hanging, and gathering with your family and friends. Well, living can be an infinite amount of different things. For my aunt, living is sitting and having tea with her friends. As my thirteen-year-old nephew will tell you, however, "video games are life." Their ideas of a living room are very far apart. As a guy who has worked with thousands of living rooms, I also believe my aunt's and my nephew's visions are two extreme possibilities of what this space can be.

For my nephew, this space is his kingdom! It's "lived in," with its big, overstuffed easy chairs, a beat-up coffee table for his feet, space to sprint when the pizza guy rings the doorbell, and maybe a basket for him to put his videogame controllers in for his mother's sake. On the other hand, for my aunt her living room is the "visiting room," and though she means it is where she sits with guests, I think she also means it is only a place she visits occasionally, because most of the time the furniture is zipped up in protective plastic coverings! The place is like a museum.

Of course those are both sort of nightmarish. The truth, though, is that in general living rooms designed by professionals are oftentimes way closer to my aunt's vision. Sure, there are no protective coverings, but professionally designed living rooms can often be too precisely designed to hold up to *life*. In my career, I've been willing to take some cues from fellas like my nephew—people who don't want to put everything back into its design-designated place each time they leave the room. (Truth be told, he's worse than that. But, he's working on it.)

To me, a "living" room should be just that, *alive*. Add life with décor that reflects the energy of you and your family. My instructions in this chapter will give you the keys to designing a stylish space that will incorporate flexibility and laid-back comfort into any style you have. And, the greatest part about not treating your perfectly decorated living room as a museum, you don't need to make any obscenely expensive acquisitions. The focus is on being affordable, durable, flexible, and stylish.

TRUE CONFESSIONS

It's probably no surprise to hear that the living room is the number one most popular space to redesign on our show. It is the heart and the center of the public portion of a home. If there is anything I've learned from designing this most popular room on a budget, it's that you need to focus on the heart of your home. We do overhaul the look of the space, but we consciously decide to make one area the focus of our efforts (and expense). Putting our most into one specific area makes the whole design pop that much more. In design-speak, this is called a focal point, but usually I consider it larger like a whole focal wall. Picking a quarter of the room—one wall and the décor positioned against it—allows us to orient the way our guests will take the space in when they first enter. The upside to this is that the design pops *every time* someone new enters it. Designing around a focal wall is a great way to prevent splurging on a full room's worth of new items and makeovers.

But don't let me mislead you. No matter how much money you have to redecorate with, your design will always be more dramatic if you anchor it around one focal point and then work outward.

Q.D.E. ALERT
function

How much living are you doing? Your living room should be comfortable, flexible, and purposely designed to make living less stressful. It should be easy to move through and have tantalizing spots where you and others feel they can relax, sink into a warm sofa, and stay for a while. Unlike Entertaining Spaces (chapter 10), it is important to determine how many people should be able to relax in the room at the same time on a daily basis. To save space and money, the design you produce will incorporate convenient storage, because that will help this room remain stylish through constant use.

DON'TS AND DOS

Don't:

* Overcompensate and crowd the space with furniture. Even if you want a lush, opulent feel to the room, it's best not to take up all your precious space with large, heavy objects.
* Orient the room and all of the seating around a television set.
* Overdesign your space along an impersonal theme. For example, don't buy a half-dozen Italian ceramics just to be *sure* your guests know that it's your "Tuscan retreat."

Do:

* Balance the room with enough seating, storage, and flair to complement your lifestyle.
* Choose a focal point for your design that expresses your personality (art, heirloom furniture, an architectural feature, or one of the included DIY projects).
* Find a flow. Leave at least three feet of clear space as a path for people to walk through.
* Choose a focal wall to be the centerpiece of your design.

A COMMON PROBLEM: BAD CIRCULATION

And I don't mean high blood pressure. I'm referring to something more sinister, stubbed toes, a.k.a. the most frustrating thing in the world! And most of the time they are the result of poor furniture placement, which affects your circulation pattern. (Rushing around in a tight space causes those devilish little collisions, too, and if you're a big guy like me, you're a bull in a china shop and may end up taking someone out.)

Still, you have to rush sometimes, and an efficient circulation pattern will make it so the living room doesn't get in your way when you don't have time to stop and relax. It will also make guests and people relaxing in the room more comfortable, because they won't feel in the way of people who pass through. In addition, on a quantum level, not paying attention to a purposeful circulation pattern in your living room can disrupt the flow of how efficient things can really be in your home and life.

DIY
COOL FOCAL WALL FRAMING

MATERIALS: 4" wide by ½" thick pieces of MDF, self-priming paint, wood fill, nails

TOOLS: chop saw or circular saw, paintbrush, paint roller, nail gun or hammer and nails, level, measuring tape

ASSEMBLY: (You can determine the amount of cross and down planks based on the budget and look you're going for: more detailed leans toward traditional; more streamlined leans toward modern.)

1. Measure the MDF and cut the strips down to size (miter the corner ends if possible; if not, straight ends are fine, too). Paint the strips and let dry.
2. Install outer frame with nails and hammer. Use the level.
3. Install inside down strips. Use the level.
4. Install cross strips (use the level to be sure your boards are straight). Use the level!
5. Fills all nail holes, sand, and paint. (I like doing a monochromatic paint look with a focal wall like this, but staining or painting the wood planks a contrasting color looks great, too!)

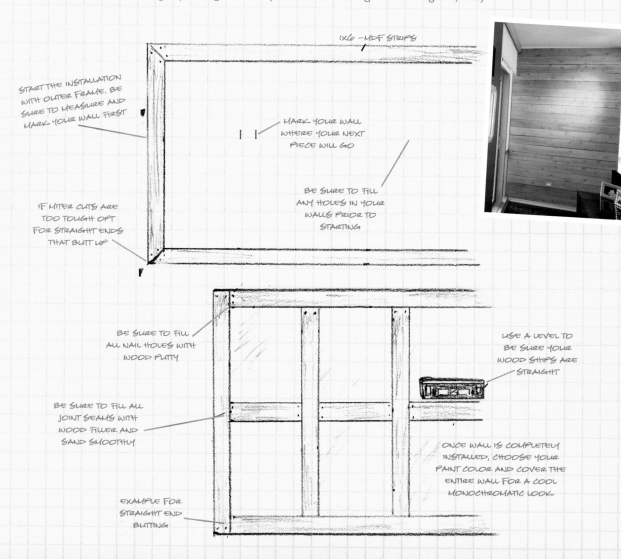

1X6 —MDF STRIPS

START THE INSTALLATION WITH OUTER FRAME. BE SURE TO MEASURE AND MARK YOUR WALL FIRST

MARK YOUR WALL WHERE YOUR NEXT PIECE WILL GO

BE SURE TO FILL ANY HOLES IN YOUR WALLS PRIOR TO STARTING

IF MITER CUTS ARE TOO TOUGH OPT FOR STRAIGHT ENDS THAT BUTT UP

BE SURE TO FILL ALL NAIL HOLES WITH WOOD PUTTY

USE A LEVEL TO BE SURE YOUR WOOD STRIPS ARE STRAIGHT

BE SURE TO FILL ALL JOINT SEAMS WITH WOOD FILLER AND SAND SMOOTHLY

ONCE WALL IS COMPLETELY INSTALLED, CHOOSE YOUR PAINT COLOR AND COVER THE ENTIRE WALL FOR A COOL MONOCHROMATIC LOOK

EXAMPLE FOR STRAIGHT END BUTTING

TAKING CONTROL OF YOUR CIRCULATION

Luckily, fixing the circulation in your room is easier than the whole "exercise and eat right" hassle we have to go through to keep our body's circulation in good shape. Here are quick steps to fix the circulation in your living room:

1. Make sure there is an obvious entry and exit to your space. Sometimes dressing the border of an entry with inexpensive decorative moldings, appliqués, fabric, or a simple painted border can draw the eye in the right direction.

2. Let the three-foot cleared path link the entry and exit with as straight a line as possible. Obviously your floor plan will vary, but the bottom line to keep in mind is try to leave as much space as possible.

3. Leave a bit more space between furniture than is necessary. This will not only open the entire space up more but blend your circulation path in while keeping it intuitive for people passing through the room.

4. Designate areas of function in your room—what I like to call "zones." If there is a sitting area, a reading nook, and a TV area, then make sure each zone can be clearly identified by how you arrange and group your furniture. Having a few feet between each zone helps break the room up.

*THE CHAIRS ARE SPACED SO THAT THERE IS A FLOW FROM ALL SIDES OF THE SITTING AREA

DIY
MAKING YOUR OWN ALTERNATIVE TO AREA RUGS

MATERIALS: latex paint in several colors, metallic paint, polyurethane

TOOLS: stencils, painter's tape, paintbrushes in various sizes

ASSEMBLY:

1. Unlike a simpler version in the kitchen, I recommend approaching a larger public space's floor "clothes" with stencils and several colors. Start with geometric and damask stencils and think of what design you'll do within a rectangular space on your floor.
2. Take measurements and sketch your design out.
3. Tape off the edges of your "canvas," and tape down your stencils. Paint enough coats of latex in your desired colors to fill the stencils.
4. Remove the stencils when the paint dries, and tape the edges of the stenciled design. Paint the larger, filler colors between the tape.
5. After the latex paint dries, use a metallic paint and a fine brush to add details and strengthen the lines in the design.
6. Allow the paint to dry, and seal the area with polyurethane or a flat varnish.

DIRTY LITTLE SECRET

YOU CONTROL THE CIRCULATION

If you are worried that your circulation path is not intuitive enough, don't worry because there is an easy fix. Throw an area rug or a runner where the path should be. I guarantee people will be drawn to it. People cannot resist walking on the right path; it's a fact of life. Especially when it's a nice soft rug. This is highly useful if the architecture of your room makes it hard for you to make the path a direct straight line between entrance and exit.

THE FOCUS OF THIS LIVING ROOM *
I DESIGNED IS ALL ABOUT THE
FAUX LEATHER WALL FABRICS

FOCUS ON YOU

Let's talk specifics about how to make a focal point in your living room. It's a good idea to have several pieces of décor that people will focus on, but you'll need to set up your seating furniture and lighting to direct attention to one. This means that for each seating area—and there can be more than one in a living room—there will be a feature of the design that you can deliberately focus on.

Furniture can complement or focus on a decorative item or feature. Angle your side seating toward it or place seating next to, underneath, or in front of it.

You don't need to angle all of the furniture. Placing the largest piece against a wall at the farthest point directly across from your focus is a good way to open a space and keep attention directed where you choose. The versatility of angling the smaller pieces is an indispensable asset for planning your living room's zones. Here are some examples of focusing using furniture.

The objects you focus attention on, as well as those that provide ambient decoration, should add your personal

vibe to the room. Aside from heirlooms and art you've collected, I find handmade and custom goods are the best way to add some of yourself into your design. And if your own hands made these items, you'll not only have an extra bit for conversation, but you'll also be reminded of what you can accomplish whenever you are in the living room. That's the number one reason I recommend trying your hand at some of these DIY projects. They could be just the thing your living room needs. (Saving lots of money is a close number two.)

SEATING AROUND A FOCAL POINT

SEATING AROUND A FIREPLACE

SEATING AROUND A COFFEE TABLE

SEATING FOR MORE SOCIAL GATHERINGS

SEATING AROUND OTTOMANS

SEATING WITH A VIEW

DIY
STYLISH, ENERGY-SAVING RADIATOR COVER

MATERIALS: One 4'x8' sheet of ¾" MDF, paint of choice, bottle of heat-resistant black spray paint, one 3' x 3' piece of decorative radiator grating

TOOLS: drill with a 2"-wide paddle bit (or doorknob drill bit—ask at your local hardware store), chop or circular saw, jigsaw, wood screws, nails, nail gun or hammer, wood glue, painter's tape, sandpaper

ASSEMBLY:

1. Measure your radiator and cut pieces of MDF slightly larger for the front, side, and top panels. Add at least 3" to the actual radiator dimensions.
2. Measure and cut large oval holes on the front and side pieces using your jigsaw.
3. Using your paddle or door knob drill bit, drill out circles on all four corners of both front and side panels (this is for ventilation purposes).
4. Sand all edges smooth.
5. Paint outside to the base color of choice.
6. Paint the inside with heat-resistant spray paint.
7. Attach your radiator grating to the back side, covering each panel hole.
8. Assemble all pieces with wood glue, nails, or screws.
9. Slide the cover over your radiator.

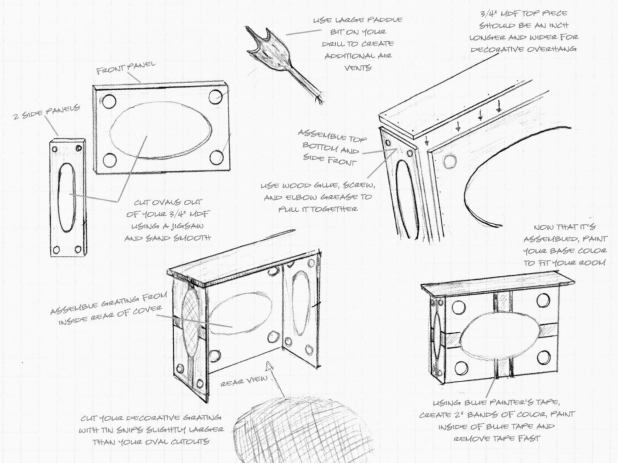

USE LARGE PADDLE BIT ON YOUR DRILL TO CREATE ADDITIONAL AIR VENTS

3/4" MDF TOP PIECE SHOULD BE AN INCH LONGER AND WIDER FOR DECORATIVE OVERHANG

FRONT PANEL

2 SIDE PANELS

ASSEMBLE TOP BOTTOM AND SIDE FRONT

USE WOOD GLUE, SCREW, AND ELBOW GREASE TO PULL IT TOGETHER

CUT OVALS OUT OF YOUR 3/4" MDF USING A JIGSAW AND SAND SMOOTH

NOW THAT IT'S ASSEMBLED, PAINT YOUR BASE COLOR TO FIT YOUR ROOM

ASSEMBLE GRATING FROM INSIDE REAR OF COVER

REAR VIEW

CUT YOUR DECORATIVE GRATING WITH TIN SNIPS SLIGHTLY LARGER THAN YOUR OVAL CUTOUTS

USING BLUE PAINTER'S TAPE, CREATE 2" BANDS OF COLOR, PAINT INSIDE OF BLUE TAPE AND REMOVE TAPE FAST

FAUX MARBLE STICKER—
NO MARBLE, NO GLUE,
NO MESS, MEANS MORE
MONEY IN MY POCKET

* BEFORE

* AN IKEA FLOATING SHELF
TURNS INTO A MANTEL
WITH JUST A FEW SCREWS

*FOR A CHEAP SOLUTION TO A LARGE MIRROR I NAILED 16 MINI MIRRORS AT $1.50 APIECE TO THE WALL FOR THIS ECLECTIC LOOK!

*ONE HOUR AND $50 LATER, WE HAVE A DOWN AND DIRTY MAKEOVER WITH DRAMATIC IMPACT.

DIY

PIMP YOUR PILLOWS FOR LESS

MATERIALS: two decorative table napkins, cotton batting

TOOLS: needle and thread (or sewing machine)

ASSEMBLY:

1. Sew three edges of each napkin to another other and stuff the pillow with cotton batting. Be sure to sew just inside the napkin's fringe or finished edge so that professional stitching shows.
2. Sew the final side shut, and enjoy your new throw pillows!

DIY

MOSAIC END TABLE

MATERIALS: old end table, old flatware plates, self-adhesive grouting, paint or stain

TOOLS: brown paper bag, hammer, trowel, paintbrush

ASSEMBLY:

1. Time to release some stress. Throw your plates in the bag and hammer away!
2. Paint or stain the legs of the table however you'd like.
3. Use the trowel to spread a layer of grouting onto the top of the table. You may want to arrange the plates first to get an idea, but randomness isn't the worst thing here.
4. Arrange the plate pieces in the grouting until the tabletop is covered. Use a piece of wood or metal to stamp it all down flat and let it sit for several hours.

WORKING WITH A SMALL SPACE

Despite how important the living room is, the life-essential nature of kitchens, bathrooms, and bedrooms means that they will have been the first considerations of whomever built your home. Especially in urban apartments, the living room might end up in a small or awkward space. If this is your situation, here are some tips to make your small space feel larger:

* Reduce the scale. Use furniture that is slimmer and shorter. Don't worry; just because your space won't allow you to have an overstuffed couch doesn't mean you have to sacrifice comfort. I recommend finding a sofa or chair that has at least a four-inch bottom cushion and a soft, durable fabric like micro-suede. The addition of lots of fluffy, decorative throw pillows will not only add a bit of color and style but can bring on the extra back support.

* Use a window as a focal point if possible. Dress it up to bring attention to it with some inexpensive appliqués, ornamented moldings, or striking fabric curtains. Drawing attention to the window will allow the room to borrow the feeling of size from the expanse of space outside.

* A large, decorative mirror can provide an ambient optical illusion that will add size to the space. Try leaning a large full-length mirror against a wall, preferably across from your main light source (the window) and watch how it bounces the light throughout your space. If you don't want to spend money on an oversized ornamental mirror, you can always DIY a plain one.

DIRTY LITTLE SECRET

MODULAR FURNITURE WORKS

Furniture that can be separated into several pieces is in vogue right now. Designers love to camouflage modular pieces in all sorts of creative ways. Modular furniture is one of the best ways to spend money on new pieces because it saves lots of space and brings tons of unique style. The possibilities, if you look online or at showrooms, are truly endless and typically quite affordable. Here are some of the best ideas I've seen:

* The classic: a couch that splits into a love seat and a chair.
* Box-style shelves that can be attached to each other in almost any formation and at different angles.
* Big circular capsules that split into two comfy chairs and a café table.
* A high coffee table that can turn into a low coffee table with three Japanese-style sitting pads, a comfy chair and side table, or a guest bed complete with a headboard and nightstand.

DIY
WOODEN CHAIR MAKEOVER

MATERIALS: stencils, latex paints, fabric paints

TOOLS: painter's tape, paintbrushes

ASSEMBLY:

1. Tape your stencils to the chair as you'd like. Remember you can layer your design.
2. Using the appropriate paint for wood or fabric, fill in the stencils with several coats of paint.
3. Strip the stencils and retouch until you love your unique new chair.

DIY
ECLECTIC STORAGE OTTOMAN

MATERIALS: two 6' long 2x4s, six pieces of ¼"-thick 1½' squares of MDF, 1½' square pieces of 3"-thick foam pad, 1 bag of cotton batting, fabric of choice, latex paint colors of choice

TOOLS: handsaw or chop saw, wood screws, drill, wood glue, jigsaw, measuring tape, spray glue, staple gun, paintbrush, stencil of choice

ASSEMBLY:

1. Using the handsaw, cut the 2x4s down to 18" pieces (size may vary based on the scale of your space).
2. Using wood screws and 2x4s, assemble a 2x4 frame.
3. Paint your six MDF square facing pieces and apply your stencil.
4. Using your jigsaw, notch out corners of the bottom MDF surface piece to fit into frame.
5. Assemble the outside facing pieces with wood screws (try counter-sinking the screws, then cover them with wood fill and paint to hide them).
6. Spray glue the 3" foam pad to the top MDF square, add batting, and staple fabric on to the underside of the MDF.
7. To keep the top piece from sliding, use adhesive to add small stabilizing strips of wood just inside the lip of the ottoman open area.
8. Stencil the side panels of the ottoman however you would like or simply leave it with a simple wood finish—you could also use a darker wood stain in the stencil instead of paint for a more subtle and organic design element.

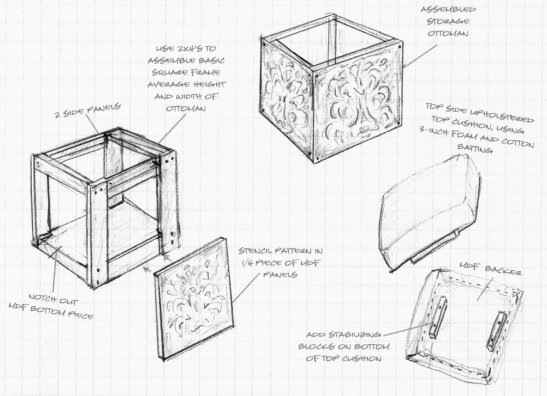

USE 2X4'S TO ASSEMBLE BASIC SQUARE FRAME AVERAGE HEIGHT AND WIDTH OF OTTOMAN

ASSEMBLED STORAGE OTTOMAN

2 SIDE PANELS

TOP SIDE UPHOLSTERED TOP CUSHION, USING 3-INCH FOAM AND COTTON BATTING

NOTCH OUT MDF BOTTOM PIECE

STENCIL PATTERN IN 1/4 PIECE OF MDF PANELS

MDF BACKER

ADD STABILIZING BLOCKS ON BOTTOM OF TOP CUSHION

* HIGHLIGHTING THE STRUCTURAL COLUMN IN THIS SPACE KICKS UP THE STYLE FOR VERY LITTLE COST

DIY
CIGAR BOX TABLETOP

MATERIALS: empty cigar boxes, amber shellac, old table

TOOLS: box cutter, paintbrush, spray-on industrial adhesive

ASSEMBLY:

1. Cut the cigar boxes so that you are left with just the tops. You'll want to lay them on the tabletop so they come to the same height; if some are thicker than others, use paper to balance the heights.
2. Adhere the cigar boxes, as flush to each other as you can, to the tabletop. (Any space between them will be filled by shellac and will even the surface out.)
3. Cut the edges of the collage to match the dimensions of the table.
4. Brush shellac over the boxes until the surface is even and the amber has given them an antiquated look.

Try this same method with other paper and cardboard images and other colors of shellac!

GO GET 'EM!

Now you're armed with some new tools and the know-how to design a living room that can be as casual and functional as you like without sacrificing an ounce of style. By paying attention to the flow of energy in this space, you will also facilitate circulation, not just through the living room but ultimately through the whole house as you pass through it on your busier days.

DIRTY LITTLE SECRET

EVERYONE HAS A SECRET STASH

Furniture can be storage, too! Or, should I say storage can be furniture? The truth is you can go in either direction. If you are looking for more space, one of the quickest solutions is to find multi-functional pieces, like an ottoman that opens up for use as a chest. Or, vice versa. You could upholster a chest or lay a soft blanket over it and use it as an ottoman. Pretty soon you'll be looking at every piece of furniture you own, wondering how you can hollow it out! Furniture that can store things is a far older concept than, say, modular furniture. That means that if you look hard enough you can find storage furniture in whatever design style you need!

PUTTING IT ALL TOGETHER
cohesion

Your living room should have a deliberate circulation pattern that allows for easy motion through the space while the rest of the room offers the temptation to stop and relax. While relaxing, people's attention should be drawn to key focal objects of the décor. The overall ambiance of the décor should be in harmony with these focal items because above all, everything should be an expression of your (and your family's) personality.

CHAPTER SEVEN

SLEEPING SPACES

Designing the Perfect Restful Nest

The bedroom is a great place to feel Q.D.E. at work. The space and energy surrounding you as you fall asleep each night and as you awake each morning is the setting of the beginning and ending of every day. Your bedroom's design and style helps contribute to that great feeling when you wake up . . . or that lousy one. If, however, you are among the many people who have trouble sleeping, don't turn to pharmaceutical sleep aids just yet. Your restlessness could be aggravated by some chaos in your bedroom environment. Clutter, piles of clothes, unseemly furniture, or some nagging vestiges of your busy daytime life can all detract from the restfulness of your sanctuary. A quick, low-budget bedroom make-over is a great way to bring new energy, harmony, and balance to your nocturnal world.

TRUE CONFESSIONS

It's in designing bedrooms that I'm so often heartbroken. Not because of what you might think happens *during* the bedroom makeover, but because there is an idea out there—one that many guests come on the show with—that makes my job very hard at times. The problem is that people just don't want to dedicate the bedroom to being a haven away from work. There's extra space that could be used for productivity, they say! Out of all the spaces in their homes, folks want work spaces, desks, and computers in their bedrooms. Let me rephrase that: People want the opposite of relaxation space in the rooms that should be dedicated to relaxation. This might be why so many people are on some kind of relaxation medication. It's wrong, I tell you, *wrong*! With that said, if you live in a really big house, and have a side room off your bedroom, or enough space to have a sense of separation from the sleeping area, then by all means, go for it. (But consult the *Office Spaces* chapter on page 153 for advice on strengthening the separation.)

I always politely insist that the bedroom stays tranquil, but often I have left a serene and stylish room after a tremendous makeover, knowing that the owners will insist on inserting a desk space for personal accounting and Internet surfing once the last camera has been hauled out. One of my hardest moments was with a homeowner who I'd had an almost spiritual discussion with about the need for serenity in her sleep space. As I was about to leave after the last day of shooting, she confessed that despite letting me go through with everything, her husband planned to move a desk and computer station—and an old beige filing cabinet!—back into the room once my team was out the door. Believe me, this bedroom would have been the envy of a Zen master, and the news was heartbreaking.

I understand it's hard for people to dedicate square footage to pure relaxation. So if you must bring work into the bedroom, a laptop can cut down on the need for a desk. But if you can help it, try to keep busywork out of the bedroom. The thing you see first and last of every day should not be your checkbook and your Facebook status. That said, let's talk about what it should be.

Q.D.E. ALERT
function

Just as you want to limit the amount of traffic your bedroom handles as a public space, you also want to limit the activeness of the design. Each aspect of your design should have the goal of relaxation. Colors should soothe, storage should aid in decluttering and have both style and multiple functions if possible, furniture layout should be simple and balanced, and décor should be expressive without being too intense. Yes, you will use the bedroom as a storage and dressing space, a setting for intimacy, and occasionally bring work into it, but the ultimate function of your bedroom is as an inviting nest to fall asleep in and a friendly, familiar place to wake up in.

DON'TS AND DOS

Don't:

* Bring the drama of your day into the bedroom. Change your design to help change your attitude.
* Use bright hues of color that make you feel a sense of urgency. (Of course, these colors will vary depending on your personal taste.)
* Overdo your design to the point where you feel as if you are sleeping in a museum. Like color, décor should lend itself to subtlety instead of intensity.
* Waste your money by being a princess or prince of pillows. Too many pillows on a bed is one of those design indulgences that aren't always pretty. Who

Do:

wants to take six pillows off their bed each night and then find a decent place to store them?

* Create a destination out of your bedroom that carries you to a calm, peaceful place. Seek inspiration from your favorite vacations.
* Work with earthy colors, and don't be afraid of dark colors, as they will aid in letting you sleep later in the morning. Keep an equal balance of design, high style, and downright warm cozy comfort.
* Include decorative pillows, but *use the rule of three for this one*. Two matching Euro-sized pillows with shams and one funky pillow that makes a statement. That's really all you need.

✳ A DEEP NAVY BLUE AND GOLD CONTRAST MAKES THIS BEDROOM GLAM!

DIY
HEADBOARDS AND ILLUSIONS

A headboard can be either the soul of a bedroom's look or the blandest part. Here is a quick rundown of my favorite ways to achieve an awesome headboard on a tight budget:

WHITEWASHING AN ANTIQUE

Find an old wood headboard with an interesting shape and whitewash it (for information on white-washing, see page 12). A bright white headboard fits great in a contemporary space even if the shape is old-fashioned. Depending on your bedding and other décor, you can dress a bright white head-board up or down.

LARGE-SCALE CANVAS ART

One large print can take the place of a headboard in an artful way. I recommend images with gentle shapes and not too many colors. This is a popular trick for staging a house when it's up for sale.

HANGING FABRIC

This headboard illusion softens the texture of your bedroom while adding any color or pattern you want! You can tack or nail the fabric directly to the wall or install a decorative curtain rod. The freedom of price and style you have in buying fabric makes this a high-impact design element for very little cash.

MIRRORS

Horizontal mirrors over the bed will highlight how central it is. A bolder look is multiple vertical mir-rors in a row over the bed.

MULTIPLE FRAMES

Grouping several framed pictures into a cluster the size of a headboard or larger will accentuate the personality of your bedroom. You can buy uniform frames and sizes or go a more eclectic route. Still-life and landscape photos are usually the best call, and the way you group them together is an oppor-tunity to express yourself and your dreams.

PIECES OF FENCING

Repurposing old fencing brings a totally different view into your sleep scene. Think about it. A rural road or field can be the most relaxing place in the world. Hang fencing with nails or French cleats.

UNCANNY ITEMS

Fencing isn't the only thing that can be brought from a different setting to add interest to the bed-room. Positioning untraditional bedroom décor in a headboard position or in close proximity to the bed can enhance the personal style of the whole room. My friend Dave has a tall ladder positioned against the wall his bed that doesn't intrude, adds charac-ter, and emphasizes the height of his ceilings.

THE BUDGET BEDROOM BASICS

Every bedroom, even those on a budget, should have a few essential items. These are usually unique to a bedroom space and are excellent places in which to concentrate your personal style. They are essential because they serve the bedroom function and allow for a unique design flow. Additionally, I have some DIY tricks to help save you a dime on your quest to get a stylish night's sleep.

The Headboard

The bed's headboard is the unsung hero of bedroom design. I like to use it as a focal point—the first thing the eye falls on when one enters the room. Unique headboards tend to come on unique bedframes, though, and thus threaten to take up your entire bedroom budget!

Beds and Bedding

First things first. Make your bed every morning. It starts your day right and allows you to end it right. Also, if you've made good design choices about a frame, sheets, pillows, blankets, and comforters, then why not display them in the way they were meant to be shown?

Buying a fancy bed frame can be difficult on a budget, which is why I recommend finding an inexpensive, unobtrusive option that will allow you to use other, less-expensive bedroom basics to enhance your style. Consider the color and finish and whether you want the solid look of a closed bottom bed or the storage space offered under a raised frame. After that, go custom with your bedding, headboard, and nightstand!

The first priority of your bedding (sheets, pillows, blankets, comforters, duvets) should be comfort. Go by touch before you start considering look. If you decide to go bold with your bedding, duvets and comforters especially, remember that it will be the largest design feature in the room. Make sure the colors, patterns, and shapes you select will work as focal points of your design.

DIRTY LITTLE SECRET

INSIDER INFO ON BEDDING DIMENSIONS

There are certain things in this world that remain difficult despite the fact that everyone wants them to be easy. Buying bedding when you don't want to purchase a prepackaged set can be one of those things. For your convenience, and in the hope that you'll mix and match your bedding, here is a sizing chart:

MATTRESS SIZES
* Twin: 39 x 75 inches (or 99 x 190 cm)
* X-Long Twin: 39 x 80 inches (99 x 203 cm)
* Full: 54 x 75 inches (137 x 190 cm)
* Queen: 60 x 80 inches (or 153 x 203 cm)
* King: 76 x 80 inches (or 198 x 203 cm)
* California King: 72 x 84 inches (or 182 x 213 cm)

FITTED SHEET SIZES
* Twin: 39 x 75 inches (or 99 x 190 cm)
* X-Long Twin: 39 x 80 inches (99 x 203 cm)
* Full: 54 x 75 inches (137 x 190 cm)
* Queen: 60 x 80 inches (or 153 x 203 cm)
* King: 76 x 80 inches (or 198 x 203 cm)
* California King: 72 x 84 inches (or 182 x 213 cm)

FLAT SHEET SIZES
* Twin: 66 x 96 inches (or 167 x 243 cm)
* X-Long Twin: 66 x 102 inches (or 167 x 259 cm)
* Full: 81 x 96 inches (or 205 x 243 cm)
* Queen: 90 x 102 inches (or 228 x 259 cm)
* King/California King: 108 x 102 inches (or 274 x 259 cm)

COMFORTER SIZES
* Twin: 68 x 86 inches (or 173 x 218 cm)
* Full/Queen: 86 x 86 inches (or 218 x 218 cm)
* King/California King: 100 x 90 inches (or 254 x 229 cm)

DIY
CONTEMPORARY HIGH HEADBOARD

MATERIALS: six pieces of 2'x2'x½" MDF squares (have them pre-cut at the store), three bags of cotton batting, 5 yards of discount fabric of choice, Two 6' long 2x4s, Three 6' pieces of 1x4 MDF or knotty pine

TOOLS: drill, staple gun, spray adhesive, chop saw or handsaw, wood glue, paint or stain (depending on desired finish), wood screws, paintbrush

ASSEMBLY:

1. Spray the adhesive on the MDF squares and wrap them with cotton batting.
2. Follow with fabric wrapped tightly over the batting. Staple the backside to the MDF (to start, put a staple in the center of each side first, than work your way around each side).
3. Once all six squares are upholstered, line them up on the ground, fabric side face down and butting up tightly to each other.
4. Attach two squares together (side by side) with small pieces of 1x4 planks by screwing through the rear of the wood using a screw just long enough to puncture the wood, about 1" deep.
5. Stain or paint your 2x4 supports.
6. Once all your 2x2 pairs of MDF are secure, line your 2x4s down the center of the backs of each row of three pads, leaving about a 3" overhang on top and bottom. Secure the pads to the 2x4 by screwing through the 2x4 the same way you did the 1x4 joiners.
7. Now your headboard is ready to be mounted to the wall with long screws that will go through the 3" top and bottoms of the 2x4s.
8. Cap the front face top and side with your remaining 1x4 pieces of wood.

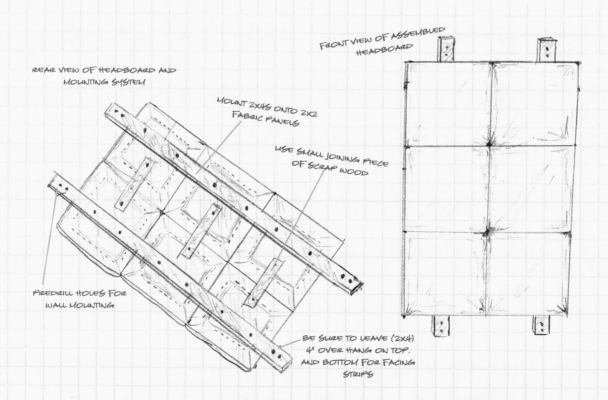

FRONT VIEW OF ASSEMBLED HEADBOARD

REAR VIEW OF HEADBOARD AND MOUNTING SYSTEM

MOUNT 2X4S ONTO 2X2 FABRIC PANELS

USE SMALL JOINING PIECE OF SCRAP WOOD

PREDRILL HOLES FOR WALL MOUNTING

BE SURE TO LEAVE (2X4) 4" OVER HANG ON TOP. AND BOTTOM FOR FACING STRIPS

DIY

DARLING DAMASK END TABLE

MATERIALS: old or inexpensive end table, white paint, spray-on industrial adhesive, black-and-white damask wallpaper, Krazy Glue

TOOLS: plastic wallpaper spreader (or plastic straightedge), paintbrush, razor

ASSEMBLY:

1. Paint the table white (or simply use a white table).
2. Spray the table surface with adhesive and, with the wallpaper still on the roll, roll it over the table while using the spreader or straightedge to smooth out air bubbles as you go.
3. When the table is covered, cut the roll free. Use the razor to trim the edges to fit the dimensions of the table.
4. Fix any frayed or peeling edges of the wallpaper with small applications of Krazy Glue.

Q.D.E. ALERT
ambiance

Ambiance in your bedroom is helped in a big way by organization. With the bed area and the necessary large storage furniture as the centers of your look, turn to décor that adds style without taking up floor space. Your space will be more relaxing if it is more open. Open spaces have ambiance, too, though. Lighting is the most important element here. With task lighting in place, turn to adjustable area lighting like dimmers to control the bedroom's ambiance. Candles are also perfect for setting the right mood.

NEAT NIGHTSTANDS LEAD TO NIRVANA

Your nightstand is too closely affiliated with your bed—the center of rest in your life—to be messy. Put some thought into basic organization on the surface, and be sure to put the few seconds needed into tidying the nightstand each day to remove clutter and chaos from your sleep setting.

DIY
CUSTOM LAMPSHADE

MATERIALS: white lampshade, one or two colors of fabric paint, stencils, fringe

TOOLS: hot glue gun

ASSEMBLY:

1. Purchase a simple white shade and two colors or tones of fabric paint for stenciling. Purchase fringe for the top and bottom of the shade.
2. Use a decorative stencil to apply the main color. Geometric stencils or small items that you can repeat in a pattern are a great idea.
3. Let all paint dry, then, using a hot glue gun, attach the fringe on the tops and bottom edges of the shade.
4. Place the shade on the light fixture and illuminate your handiwork!

The Nightstand

Talk about multipurpose! Nightstands and end tables will handle your books, clocks, tissues, and other essentials while you sleep, but that doesn't mean you should treat them as a dumping ground. Find a nightstand with drawers or, if it's more of a table with full legs, place a basket or other nice-looking container below for stowing bulkier bedside items.

Task Lamps

Two task lamps are a necessity if you share your bed with a partner. Everyone needs to be a night owl sometimes. Price will tempt you into buying the most generic lamps possible, but I encourage you to match the design style of your bedroom. A great lampshade will provide style for a lifetime.

Wardrobe Containment

A bedroom should provide ample space to store your clothes, shoes, jewelry, and miscellaneous stuff. Furniture designers have focused on wardrobe solutions for ages, so you'll have nearly infinite choices. By default, you'll want drawer space and hanger space in addition to something that conceals them. This can be a full armoire—don't think you can't afford one until you browse flea markets and the Internet. It can also be a dresser, chest of drawers, built-in closet . . . any combination of drawers and doors. If you're strapped for storage space, consider storing shoes and occasional items under the bed.

DIY
CLOSET MIRROR CONVERSION

MATERIALS: old mirrored sliding closet door, MDF crown molding, ¼" furring strips

TOOLS: industrial-strength adhesive, handsaw (or chop saw), miter box (if you're cutting 45-degree angles), clamps, screwdriver (or drill), measuring tape, paintbrush

ASSEMBLY:
1. Remove all screws and hardware from bottom and top of mirror.
2. Adhere furring strips to inside edge of mirror (clamp and let dry).
3. Cut MDF crown molding down to size of the door's dimensions, paint, and glue to furring strips and frame (clamp and let dry).

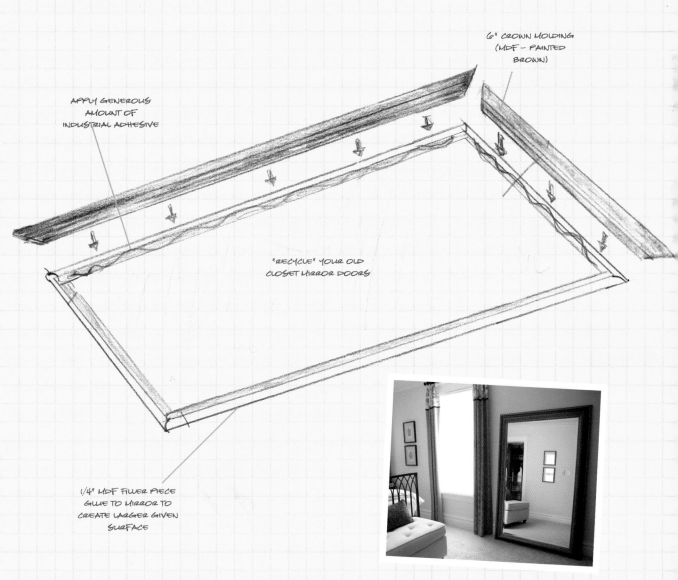

6" CROWN MOLDING
(MDF – PAINTED BROWN)

APPLY GENEROUS AMOUNT OF INDUSTRIAL ADHESIVE

"RECYCLE" YOUR OLD CLOSET MIRROR DOORS

¼" MDF FILLER PIECE GLUE TO MIRROR TO CREATE LARGER GIVEN SURFACE

A COMMON PROBLEM: COLLATERAL CLOSET DAMAGE

Closet organization and the closet customization business is a multimillion-dollar industry. Yes, there are people who will come to your home and professionally fold and put away your stuff for a large fee. But there is no need to go to that extreme. Here are four foolproof, low-budget ways to create some space and sanity in your closet.

1. Purge

Wardrobes change—ditch the stuff that no longer makes the cut. The leather pants from 1982, the sixteen pairs of old sneakers, and most of the clothes you have not worn in more than two years. You'll be amazed at how much we really do wear . . . it's not as much as you think. Feel good about cleaning out your closet by never bringing it to the dumpster. Donate old clothes to younger family members or Goodwill. Remember, tax rebates are available!

2. Store like Spider-Man

Use concealed wall space and the backs of closet doors for storage. Add additional shelves in closets wherever possible. Use simple shelf kits that have L-brackets, shelves, anchors, and screws in one package. Also, take advantage of the wasted space behind the door with a shoe rack that hangs from the door top—there is nothing as easy to install.

3. Repurpose standing shelves

Narrow bookshelves are a great thing to place in a closet. If your hanging items only cover half the empty space in the closet, why not turn that other space into storage? Cubby space is better than empty space in closets.

4. Find the ultimate storage space

The best organizer I know is my friend Marcy. She dedicated a small room in her home to being a dressing room and laundry closet for her kids. I've never seen a home with children so naturally neat as Marcy's. This is a very out-of-the-box solution to closet space. By turning a room into a massive walk-in closet, Marcy freed up floor and storage space all throughout the house.

HERE AN OLD WOODEN LADDER MAKES A GREAT TIE RACK *

DIRTY LITTLE SECRET

CLOSET INVESTMENT PAYS OFF

There will always be cheaper solutions than a large standing armoire or wardrobe. From a designer's perspective, though, so much style and ambiance can be brought by a single large wardrobe piece that it's worth it. Decreasing the number of containers you have for your clothes frees up open space. It's also easier to base the cohesion of your style around one central object than to coordinate the look of several pieces of furniture. Finally, painting or refinishing a big old armoire will tighten your design style and provide a sense of achievement as you get ready each morning.

HAVING PHOTOGRAPHS OVER YOUR KIDS CLOSET AREA IS A GREAT PERSONAL TOUCH

*

LAUNDRY ROOM

*
CHECK OUT THE REPURPOSED BANK VAULT CLOSET

CHILDREN'S BEDROOMS

Adults have the run of the whole house, so kids need their bedrooms to be their own world in addition to a rest space. (Kids also rest a whole lot less than most of us.) A kid's bedroom should be a space that ignites the imagination and soothes the soul of the child sleeping and playing in it. Faux finishes and fun hand-painted embellishments can be a fun design element! Color splashes and stencils (see pages 12–13) are great ways to bring whimsy and personality to your child's space.

Updating the personality of a kid's room as the years go by is one of the most rewarding ways to keep your home in harmony with your family. When they are old enough, encourage your kids not only to help you with painting and redecorating but also with brainstorming and designing.

* WHIMSICAL PAINT
TECHNIQUES ADD
CHARACTER AND FUEL
IMAGINATION

The bedroom is one of the most unique spaces in the house. It has furniture found nowhere else. Its function as a place for rest and relaxation depends more on design than anything else. Yet, it's popular these days to add functions from productive daily life into the restive space—that defeats the whole point. I hope you now have the motivation to dedicate your bedroom to being a sanctuary.

Use the unique furnishings in the bedroom to add a calm, personal ambiance to the space. Bring in original, uncommon items to a bedroom with the knowledge that they will bring the highest amount of style because they are unusual—as long as they don't clutter.

PUTTING IT ALL TOGETHER
cohesion

A better bedroom means a better day, every day. Help yourself out by keeping serenity in and chaos out. This doesn't amount to any incredible spiritual experience. It's a matter of identifying the things that help you relax and incorporating them into your bedroom. Design a bed you love, use interesting and space-saving furniture, and fill the rest of your bedroom with calming light, soothing darkness, and sweet dreams.

THE VINTAGE IRON
CHANDELIER AND
* PATTERNED CURTAINS
COMPLETE THIS BEDROOM
SITTING AREA

CHAPTER EIGHT

KITCHENS

Whip Up a High-Style Tasty Space

In my family, the most popular place in the house has always been the kitchen. You might think that means there are some major obesity issues in the Fontana clan, but that's not the case. There sure is plenty of cooking at all times of day, but the majority of the time we spend in and around the kitchen is dedicated to relaxing and chatting more than chewing. The waft of stewing meatballs, broiling garlic bread, simmering minestrone soup, or slowly baking lasagna certainly does do its part to keep everyone close by the kitchen.

So what do you need to set the kitchen up for? For cooking, of course, but that's not even half of the story. You'll want space for visitors while you cook—who wants to cook alone for hours? Having extra hands isn't half-bad, either. You want your kitchen to accommodate company for longer durations than the time it takes to prepare and cook meals. If your kitchen is too small altogether, you'll want an adjacent space to facilitate a flow of good tastes, smells, and conversation. This means that comfort and style are far more important than you might think. Regarding the kitchen, you need to go beyond what's useful into what's beautiful.

TRUE CONFESSIONS

Kitchens are never an easy makeover project to pull off on TV, especially on a thousand-dollar budget! There are so many big obstacles to tackle, but when you add the challenge of emotions and personal memories to a project, things really can get tricky. Here's the scenario. I was asked to design a kitchen for a nice young couple who wanted a European/Tuscan-influenced design to transform their dated, '50s-style kitchen. They had tons of space, a great layout, and existing wood cabinets. Since we don't have the budgets to buy new appliances or install granite counters, the big wow factor in the makeover was going to come from the dramatic changes to the finish and style of the wood cabinets. That was the plan, until I found out that one of our guest's recently deceased father had built every piece of wood cabinetry in the kitchen with his own bare hands. She did not want us to disrupt the integrity of his work.

As you can imagine, it threw a kink in the plan of painting, faux finishing, or restaining the wood cabinets.

Tenderhearted designer that I am, I couldn't bring myself to convince her to update the cabinets. But, the show must go on! So, I did a little research, looking for ways to achieve the design style they'd requested without changing the charm of the cabinets. We came to a perfect consensus. Instead of replacing or painting, we rejuvenated the natural maple color of dad's work with a special polishing product. We added new rustic knobs and topped the upper cabinets with a nice crown molding to add a bit of flair. We also removed one set of doors to create a European-style exposed cabinet effect. Finally, new under-and over-the-cabinet puck lights showcased the original hard work that went into the cabinetry.

In the end, we managed to pull off the kitchen design they requested while keeping the integrity of our guest's father's work. When the tears flowed from the homeowner's eyes as she entered the kitchen, I knew we hit the mark. Improving a personal element of a space has much more value than simply seeking the new and shiny.

Q.D.E. ALERT
function

The kitchen should not be disconnected from the network of the rest of the house. You want your design to facilitate this connection. The best cooking and eating spaces have an easy flow between them. This is obvious, but always be sure these two spaces are immediately connected. There should be no need to walk through a non-food-related space when serving. Each place should have both room to maneuver and room to relax. Our goal with the kitchen is to not only make it a great-looking place to cook, but also a place to cook with lots of company.

DON'TS AND DOS

Don't:

* Allow your décor to interfere with your movement as you work in the kitchen.
* Focus on quantity of kitchen gadgets over quality and style for the essentials.
* Clash your cabinets and counters just because one look—granite countertops, for example—seems to be more popular or expensive.
* Leave storage space unused or worse, unusable.

Do:

* Use paints and finishes that are resilient against liquids and stains.
* Unify the color and design style of what you purchase for your kitchen and alter the generic elements for the space to match your theme.
* Know your design well enough to easily pick the item that fits the look of *your* kitchen when given a variety of choices.
* Seek to maintain an easy social flow between the kitchen and the adjacent room.

A COMMON PROBLEM: KNOWING THE METHOD

As huge as the impact of a kitchen with custom style is, that doesn't mean you can forget about making the space as efficient as possible. Anything that makes cooking easier will save time and money because it will encourage you to cook more frequently—and your meals will become more delicious and less expensive. There is a simple science to kitchen arrangements.

The University of Illinois developed the concept of the kitchen work triangle in the 1950s after they conducted a study to find the most sensible kitchen layout for a four-person home. They developed the triangle, connecting the critical three work areas in a kitchen: the sink, the oven, and the refrigerator.

According to this theory, the distance between each area should be no less than 4 feet and no larger than 9 feet. The three sides of the triangle, when added together, should total no more than 26 feet. For our purposes, these

numbers are only a slight recommendation. Many kitchens, especially in small urban apartments, don't provide enough space for four feet between the three stations! Still, it helps to have a rule of thumb.

There has also been a major update since the study. Most homes now have a dishwasher. The solution here is to pair the dishwasher with the sink. Most layouts follow one of these common forms:

The Single-Wall Kitchen

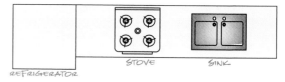

REFRIGERATOR   STOVE   SINK

The L-Shaped Kitchen

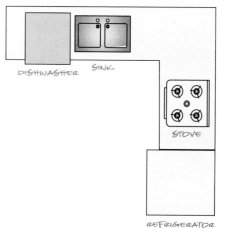

DISHWASHER   SINK

STOVE

REFRIGERATOR

The U-Shaped Kitchen

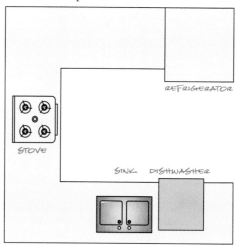

REFRIGERATOR

STOVE

SINK   DISHWASHER

Q.D.E. ALERT
ambiance

So much of a kitchen's look comes with it when you buy or rent it: the countertops, the cabinetry, and the appliances. This situation makes it so that when you purchase new items—small appliances, cutlery and cutting boards, silverware, bowls, plates, etc.— you either need to match them to the themes you're stuck with, or clash. This is all the worse because so many of the staple items you buy come in a variety of colors and looks. The end result of this process is that so many kitchens look so much alike or look like totally random collections of stuff with no design. If you value originality in your décor, why should you be stuck with so few possibilities in the place you cook? The ambiance in your kitchen should be made strong by tightly connecting themes like color and texture—precisely because 99 percent of kitchens don't have a strongly connected theme. I'll provide you with the tips and tricks to allow you to turn generic kitchen features into décor that fits your theme to a T.

The Galley Kitchen

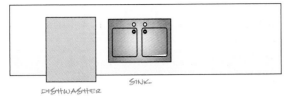

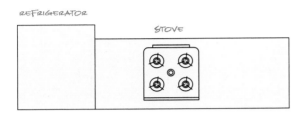

The Island-Anchored Kitchen

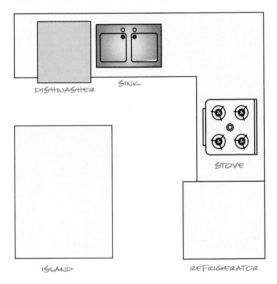

If you are working with a new or recently gutted space, keep these efficient layouts in mind.

DIRTY LITTLE SECRET

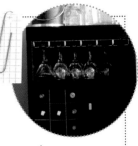

BRING THE ISLAND HOME

Are you looking at these layouts and feeling jealous of the extra counter space and storage space provided by an island? There are ways to grab those benefits without actually contracting a professional to install an island for thousands of dollars. You don't even need all that much floor space. Mobile islands are an excellent way to add size to your kitchen. Keep it about as tall as your counters so you can pull it right up to them and so it is tall enough for guests to sit at on stools. The more height it has, the more shelves or racks you can install for a huge boost of storage space. If your kitchen can't support more than a couple people, you can move the island through the doorway and you'll have a great serving space and further increase the connection between the kitchen and the adjacent space.

DIY:
THOUSAND-DOLLAR KITCHEN COUNTERS FOR LESS

MATERIALS: Skim Stone product, primer, and sealer

TOOLS: trowel, sandpaper

ASSEMBLY:

1. Skim Stone requires some waiting between coats, but the end result is incredible. Make sure your surface is clean and dry before applying a thin layer of primer with the trowel. Wait about 4 hours then sand the coat to smoothness, following it with another coat of primer.

2. Wait 8 hours for the primer to set. Apply three to four coats of Skim Stone, sanding between each and waiting 4 hours for each to dry. (It's worth the wait!)

3. Apply four to six coats of sealer, sanding between for optimum sheen. After lots of waiting and not too much effort, you'll have countertops that look like a thousand bucks.

*AFTER

TAKE CONTROL OF YOUR OTHER STATIONS

The cutting and prep station is an essential work spot that is not accounted for in the triangle idea. Neither is the spot where you'll keep your most useful small appliance (a mixer, in many cases). These are not in the triangle because they are not necessarily built in. This means that the cutting station, focused around the cutting board, and the main small appliance are the parts of your work path that you can control. I'll use the common layouts to provide my favorite examples for locating these two other stations. In placing these two stations, keep in mind that they can be messy, so if possible keep them a foot or so away from hard-to-clean spots like the stovetops and any gaps between the counter and refrigerator. Keeping in mind that many households have more than one chef, I'll also provide ideas for placing an auxiliary prep station.

The single-wall kitchen

Between the stove and the sink is the best spot for the main cutting station for the easy adding of ingredients to stovetop pots and pans. Placing the mixer between the sink and the wall is great, and then your auxiliary cutting station can be on the other side of the stove. Talk about teamwork!

The L-shaped kitchen

The corner is often the best spot for both your small appliance and your cutting station. I prefer keeping the cutting station closest to the stove and the small appliance in the next closest spot. When not in use, push the appliance back deeper into the corner to make room for an auxiliary cutting station.

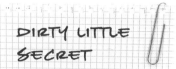
MEASURE TWICE . . .

The kitchen, because of cabinetry, makes vertical space more precious than usual. When purchasing countertop appliances, pay attention to all their dimensions—height especially. For tall items like a mixer, you'll want to be careful that you can stow it deep in the counter, under the cabinets, when it is not in use. You shouldn't own any small appliances that are taller than the height between your counter and your lowest cabinet.

The U-shaped kitchen

Here I find that either placing the cutting station in a kitty-corner position relative to the stove (so a 90-degree turn is all that is required between them) is best. If you have space, provide some empty counter spanning from the cutting board away from the stove, then place your small appliance. An auxiliary space for cutting will most likely be available next to the sink.

The galley kitchen

This parallel layout best serves your cutting station by placing it next to or across from the stove, depending on the location of the sink. In smaller apartments this layout can sometimes result in narrow strips of counter: the perfect spot for your small appliance. If you have a choice, place the auxiliary cutting station next to the sink instead of the refrigerator.

The island-anchored kitchen

The island is the indisputable champion when it comes to offering in-kitchen space for visitors. Place your main cutting station at a corner to enhance the amount of productive chatting time you can have. Place a second cutting board adjacent to the main one when you want to take advantage of extra help, but leave the space clear otherwise. Keep the small appliance off the island except on a temporary basis; tucking it in a corner and placing it next to the sink for use is a great strategy.

CUSTOMIZING YOUR KITCHEN

Until now we've mostly discussed how to work with and around parts of your kitchen that are highly expensive to alter. Well, you can give this room a major makeover without hiring a contractor. With a combination of crafty tweaks, you can make your kitchen both more stylish and more efficient. You'll need to choose a theme; think along the lines of your chosen design style and use color as your primary adjustment. Consider everything: walls (think of the general walls, the walls between counters and cabinets, and the wall behind your stovetop as three distinct areas); countertops; cabinetry; floors; appliances; and all general décor. All of this can be altered without being renovated. Let's really bring the style!

GALLEY KITCHENS LIKE THIS LEND THEMSELVES WELL TO MODERN DESIGN AND CONDO LIVING *

THREE DESIGN
STYLES TO RULE THEM ALL

Kitchen design follows three staple design styles: Modern, Rustic European, and Traditional. The idea is that these styles can pair with any design style found throughout a home. If this idea sounds suspect, rest assured that you can use color, accessories, and faux finishes to fine-tune the harmony between your kitchen and the rest of your home.

MODERN KITCHENS

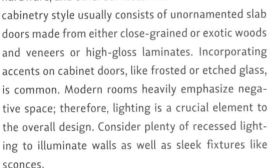

As with other Modern spaces, clean lines and bold and sleek materials typify the Modern-style kitchen. Stainless steel is a popular finish for appliances, hardware, and other surfaces. The cabinetry style usually consists of unornamented slab doors made from either close-grained or exotic woods and veneers or high-gloss laminates. Incorporating accents on cabinet doors, like frosted or etched glass, is common. Modern rooms heavily emphasize negative space; therefore, lighting is a crucial element to the overall design. Consider plenty of recessed lighting to illuminate walls as well as sleek fixtures like sconces.

RUSTIC EUROPEAN KITCHENS

This style covers design styles that are heavier and more ornamented than those supported by a Traditional kitchen; it's like the difference between Baroque and Rococo styles (pages 40–41). The architectural materials used in Rustic European style are mainly stone, raw wood, and plaster. Cabinetry often has inset doors with raised or beaded panels and cast-iron joinery. You can rusticate your look by distressing materials or using dark wood grain faux finishes (see page 13). Rustic European kitchens tend to have large, heavy moldings. Hardware is often rod-iron, pewter, or bronze. Glazed ceramic tiles in unique and creative patterns are largely common for backsplashes. Consider accessorizing with earthenware dishes and bowls. For additional charm, add a suspended pot rack centered over your island.

TRADITIONAL KITCHENS

The Traditional kitchen is considered classic and timeless. Elements emphasize quality craftsmanship and understated elegance; it is ornamented less and more lightly than a Rustic Traditional kitchen. Balance and symmetry are prominent qualities of this style. Traditional spaces provide a sense of warmth and can be extremely inviting atmospheres. Medium to light woods, polished metal joinery, and stone countertops are most common. Traditional kitchens work well as an elegant frame for accessories and so can very easily be brought into harmony with any design style, between the ornamentation of the Rustic European style and the stark lines of Modern styling.

DIY
TILING THE WALL BEHIND YOUR STOVE

MATERIALS: mortar bed, tile, cement mortar

TOOLS: trowel, level, straightedge, ledger

ASSEMBLY:

1. Apply mortar bed to the area and follow the manufacturer's curing instructions.
2. Measure your tiles and, using a level and straightedge, pencil horizontal rows for the whole area to be tiled.
3. Starting from the bottom, apply a row's worth of mortar to the area and apply tiles, pressing each into the mortar as you apply. Use the ledger to support tiles as you apply them and then to press them into the mortar.
4. Continue until the whole area is tiled and allow the tiles to set for a full day before using the stove.

Walls

It is common knowledge that white is a bad color for kitchen walls because it can look dirty so easily, and a cook cannot avoid splashes and spills on occasion. Commonly, kitchens instead receive pale wall colors: light yellows, greens, tans, and almonds are very popular. But we're trying to avoid being generic! If you're going to stray from white, don't be afraid to stray boldly. Darker, stronger colors can be incorporated into any design style if done carefully. Try two different colors or shades on the main walls and on the walls between the cabinets and counters (try using a color from the adjacent room for one of these) and see how much everything changes! Be sure to use semi-gloss paint because it is easy to clean and won't be permeated by liquids and other food spills.

Countertops

Countertops are among the most expensive upgrades available for a kitchen. The fact is that they, along with cabinetry, offer the most dramatic changes to the look of a kitchen. That is why faux finishes that are meant for cheap countertops are among the most popular. See the pictures in my Dirty Little Secret about the top kitchen styles (page 143) for profiles of the most popular faux finishes for countertops.

Cabinetry

Cabinet space tends to control what we put in our kitchens. You can take control! Try altering the shelving in your cabinets to fit your needs. Adding lots of shelves to one cabinet so it has lots of short shelves is a great way to consolidate all of your small items and clear up space for another cabinet to handle taller goods. In modern kitchens, where you don't want to intrude on space that could otherwise be empty, hanging shelves, racks, and hooks inside cabinet doors is a great way to keep your walls sleek. Adjusting cabinet shelving is the best way to accommodate objects hung on the inner doors.

DIY
ADDING MORE DIVIDERS AND
WINE GLASS STORAGE TO CABINETS

MATERIALS: MDF squares, wood glue, paint, metal-wire wine rack

TOOLS: hammer, circular saw, sandpaper, nails

ASSEMBLY:

1. Paint the MDF squares to match the inside of your cabinetry.
2. Hang a store-bought metal-wire wine glass holder to the top inside roof of the highest cabinet you have.
3. On the lower shelves, measure and cut down then add the MDF painted partitions. Apply glue to the edges and fit snugly in place (wipe off excess glue).
4. Once in place, nail the squares from both the top down and the bottom up.

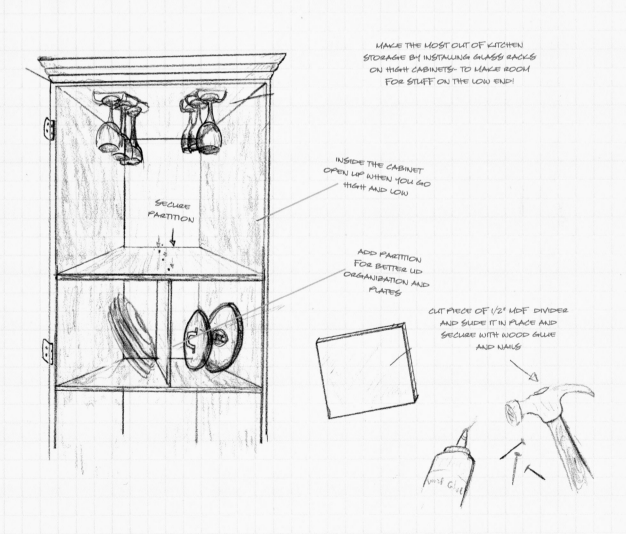

MAKE THE MOST OUT OF KITCHEN STORAGE BY INSTALLING GLASS RACKS ON HIGH CABINETS- TO MAKE ROOM FOR STUFF ON THE LOW END!

INSIDE THE CABINET OPEN UP WHEN YOU GO HIGH AND LOW

SECURE PARTITION

ADD PARTITION FOR BETTER UD ORGANIZATION AND PLATES

CUT PIECE OF 1/2" MDF DIVIDER AND SLIDE IT IN PLACE AND SECURE WITH WOOD GLUE AND NAILS

DIY
RECYCLED WINDOW POT RACK

MATERIALS: old decorative window or stained glass window with thin wood frame, old towel bars (to match the style of window—go to salvage yards for funky options), paint (optional depending on finish of window), four small eye hooks, one large eye hook, four S-hooks, thin strong chain

TOOLS: drill, sandpaper, stud finder, screws

ASSEMBLY:

1. If needed, paint the window frame the desired color or employ dry brushing to make it look older.
2. On the top side, screw in four eye hooks into the corners.
3. On the bottom side, screw on four to five towel bars, evenly spaced.
4. Flip the window back over and, using small S-hooks, attach four equal length piece of chain to match the height you wish to achieve for the pot rack (typically a foot above the top of your head is fine).
5. Using your stud finder, locate the beam in the ceiling and screw your large eye hook into it.
6. Hang your new pot rack and enjoy your decorative new space saver.

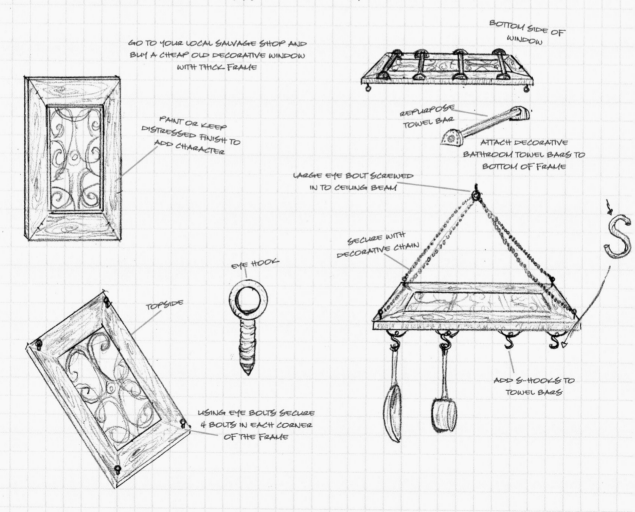

GO TO YOUR LOCAL SALVAGE SHOP AND BUY A CHEAP OLD DECORATIVE WINDOW WITH THICK FRAME

PAINT OR KEEP DISTRESSED FINISH TO ADD CHARACTER

BOTTOM SIDE OF WINDOW

REPURPOSE TOWEL BAR

ATTACH DECORATIVE BATHROOM TOWEL BARS TO BOTTOM OF FRAME

LARGE EYE BOLT SCREWED IN TO CEILING BEAM

EYE HOOK

SECURE WITH DECORATIVE CHAIN

TOPSIDE

USING EYE BOLTS SECURE 4 BOLTS IN EACH CORNER OF THE FRAME

ADD S-HOOKS TO TOWEL BARS

S

Floors

Kitchen floors are universally either tile or highly glossed wood. This is necessary to prevent damage and staining from spills. Putting a rug in a kitchen can be a tough decision and is too

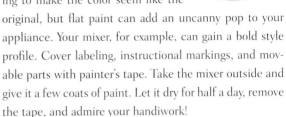

often resolved with a cheap rug that might be thrown out soon or drain money by needing frequent cleanings. Floor clothes are a versatile and popular new design element that can add color and pattern to your floor while keeping it as easy to clean as if it were naked. Using a color and pattern that fits the look of a room adjacent to the kitchen is a great idea for bringing the two spaces closer together.

Appliance and General Décor

This encompasses everything that has a visible profile in your kitchen or on your dinner table. Try to unify at least half of these things. Small appliances are almost always available with colored accents; if not, try some simple spray painting. Make sure you use paint that bonds to metal or plastic (the can will tell you); you'll want glossy paint if you're looking to make the color seem like the original, but flat paint can add an uncanny pop to your appliance. Your mixer, for example, can gain a bold style profile. Cover labeling, instructional markings, and movable parts with painter's tape. Take the mixer outside and give it a few coats of paint. Let it dry for half a day, remove the tape, and admire your handiwork!

Cutlery, on-counter storage (like jars for coffee and cooking utensils), wall-hung storage (like spice racks and hooks for pots and pans), teakettles, and flatware can all be bought in a variety of styles and colors. The kitchen doesn't have much space for non-functional décor, but what you use should do the job of adding a shape or design theme that function-driven items cannot do.

DIY
FLOOR CLOTHES FOR YOUR KITCHEN OR PETS

MATERIALS: latex paint, metallic paint, polyurethane

TOOLS: painter's tape, paintbrushes, wood graining rocker

ASSEMBLY:

1. I love using black latex paint and silver metallic for the accent. Tape and paint the latex in the shape you want—maybe a rectangle the size of a floor mat for starters. (This is great as a mat to put pet food and water bowls on.)
2. After the latex paint dries, use the graining rocker to create metallic grain marks across the latex area.
3. Allow the paint to dry and seal the area with polyurethane.

LIGHTING

Lighting in a kitchen should not be sparse. At the same time, keeping control with dimmers and smaller fixtures is beneficial because you don't always want the kitchen illuminated at cooking level. Think about coming down for a midnight snack and knowing that you have to deal with the blinding glare from powerful overhead lights that are your only fixtures in the kitchen—that alone is reason for *me* to install dimmers, but maybe you make fewer late-night kitchen raids than I do.

Another lighting idea to consider is under the cabinet lighting; use puck lights or bars of thin task lighting that you attach to the underside of cabinets. This type of dramatic lighting is more common in newer homes. It is soft and ambient, but useful, and will make the kitchen seem like a more social and romantic space in the evening. Under-cabinet lighting can allow you to forget dimmers and become the perfect guide to a midnight snack.

GO GET 'EM!

I hope you're now equipped with the knowledge to give your kitchen the makeover it deserves. Don't let everything in this room be generic—what used to require thousands of dollars in renovations can now be accomplished for a fraction of the cost. You should pay attention to little things like color decisions in utensils, flatware, and appliances because you'll now have a style theme in mind where there was nothing but a desire for efficiency before. With all these small projects at your fingertips, never think that there isn't a way to make your kitchen an easier and more pleasing place to cook.

PUTTING IT ALL TOGETHER
cohesion

Now you can avoid the trap of having a kitchen like everybody else. Employing a visible color theme, supported by items like appliances that no one ever considers style points, will add miles of style to your kitchen. Change décor-only aspects like wall accessories to pick up on themes in the rest of the house—most importantly the adjacent room. Use uncanny flourishes like floor clothes, wall-tiling, and faux finishes to expand your style profile. By redesigning the room that everyone writes off as stuck in a store-bought, bland style, you can show off your decorating mastery!

JUST OUTSIDE THE DUNNE'S
KITCHEN THEY JOIN TOGETHER
AN EATING STATION WITH
UNIFYING COLORS

*

DUNNE

CHAPTER NINE

OFFICE SPACES

Your Sanctuary for Success

This is a really important and relevant chapter to me. Two major changes have happened to the idea of the home office in today's world. For one thing, having a work space at home is way more possible these days. There are so many times that even people with everyday office jobs don't go to the office every day. With e-mail and other Internet tools, many people are able to work from home *without* faking a sick day (even though we still do it sometimes). Others only occasionally drop by the office. A rapidly growing number of folks have no office *except* in their home. As one of those folks who actually work from my "live-work-loft," I know the importance of having a space that allows you to focus on work, inspires you, and provides functional aspects geared toward your specific field of work. For me, ample drawing surface, storage, and general space to lay out my ideas are crucial to my success. Thus, I know what specifics to design for.

It's funny—if you watch old TV shows like *The Brady Bunch*, *Leave It to Beaver*, *Bewitched*, and others, you see that the idea of home offices used to be geared toward highly paid executives, lawyers, doctors, and bankers. Now they are available to, and often necessary for, a much wider range of careers. When you think of a home office, don't think you have to drop thousands upon thousands on a mahogany desk, a high-backed leather chair, fountain pen, etc. I want you to think of it as a dedicated space—it does not at all need to be a whole room—that is designed to be a tremendous upgrade over a desk; not necessarily in size or cost but in designating the function of this space as a spot to be productive.

My job is highly mobile, so I certainly do lots of work from my home office. The main problem with the setup, I know from experience, is distraction. It's tough focusing only on work when the rest of your life is so close by, like my little black 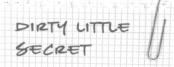 pug Stewie, who (as cute as he is) can be a big attention hog when nibbling at my ankles or jumping on my lap for his afternoon nap. So, home office placement, layout, and décor should all be geared toward inspiration and serenity, but above all creating a space that allows you to focus.

Q.D.E. ALERT
function

Your home office should be far more comfortable and more personal than a company office. Typically, when a company designs its office it focuses only on utility, and when finally it comes to pleasing the people who work for them, even companies who care have to please so many tastes that they play it safe, or as I call it: bland, boring, and blah! That's why working from home can be a beautiful thing; you can and should have total control over what materials, colors, and art surrounds you while you work. Your office should function as its own space but, even if it is not its own room, it should not interfere with other people in the house by making them stay away from a whole area just because you are working in part of it. One great way to do this is to position storage solutions as spatial dividers.

DIY
PICTURE BOX STORAGE CUBBIES

MATERIALS: five pieces of 1' 1x4 pine or MDF, a 12"x12" wood picture frame, paint, two small butterfly hinges, photo (large enough to fit frame)

TOOLS: drill, hammer or nail gun, nails, screws, chop saw, measuring tape, level

ASSEMBLY:

1. Take 4 of your 1x4 pieces of wood and assemble a basic square the same size as your wood picture frame (approximately 12"x12"). You may have to cut ¼" off the ends of your top and bottom pieces for your measurements to meet exactly 12"x12".
2. Sand and fill all nail or screw holes.
3. Use the last 1x4 and small scraps of the others as mounting brackets to the inside, back, top and bottom portions of the box. Nail these together from outer sides. Drill holes for mounting.
4. Attach the picture frame to the wood box with butterfly hinges and small screws on top of the box.
5. Paint the box and frame your color of choice (I recommend either blending them into the wall color or contrasting them with the accent color of the room).
6. Insert your photo and mount it to the wall using screws through the back mounting plates.

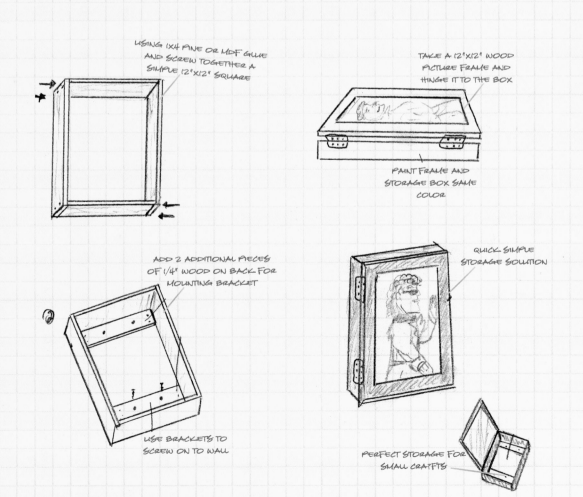

USING 1X4 PINE OR MDF GLUE AND SCREW TOGETHER A SIMPLE 12"X12" SQUARE

TAKE A 12"X12" WOOD PICTURE FRAME AND HINGE IT TO THE BOX

PAINT FRAME AND STORAGE BOX SAME COLOR

ADD 2 ADDITIONAL PIECES OF 1/4" WOOD ON BACK FOR MOUNTING BRACKET

USE BRACKETS TO SCREW ON TO WALL

QUICK SIMPLE STORAGE SOLUTION

PERFECT STORAGE FOR SMALL CRAFTS

TRUE CONFESSIONS

I once had a guest on my show ask me if I could put a home office in her dining room. As I scratched my head in wonder, my stomach turned, because I wanted to barf at the idea. A dining room is the last place I would put a home office. Uh-oh! My producers had already written the concept of "Home Office in the Dining Room" as part of the show's storyline! Thus, the difference between designing a room for a TV show and one in real life. I would never make that recommendation, but I can't tell you how many times a homeowner on a show wants to squeeze blood from stone. I'm good, but I'm not God. Ten functions in one space is a tall order! The number one request is frequently—in addition to a place to sit and read, eat, watch TV, fold laundry, work out—"can you also create a home office space too?" Let's not forget . . . all for one thousand dollars! Yeesh! As the people-pleaser my mom has taught me to be—and because my contract requires me to follow the show's storylines—I put my personal feelings aside and try to appease every crazy request I receive. Still, if you want a home office it's best to place it at the top of the multi-function request list.

DON'TS AND DOS

Don't:

* Locate your office area where it can interfere with social spaces in your home.
* Keep a cluttered, messy desk for all your guests to observe.
* Use overbearing décor that will distract more than soothe and motivate. Keep the TV in the other room, unless it's part of your job requirement.
* Make your office at home feel too much like your other office. Leave harsh lights and sterilizing styling for the hospitals.

Do:

* Provide yourself with basic office supplies to keep the work flowing.
* Find a quiet space for your office that will allow you to forget about it when you only want to relax. Conversely, put the dog in the kennel when serious work needs to be completed.

* Use closed-storage, multi-functional, and organizational furniture to keep the things you need easily in reach but not constantly exposed.
* Use items like privacy screens, curtains, and solid dividers to separate your focus from the rest of the house (if you don't have a dedicated room).
* Add personal style to your office furnishings that inspire creativity and success.

A COMMON PROBLEM: KEEPING YOUR HEAD IN THE GAME

You know those posters? The ones with a cougar jumping over a ravine and the words DETERMINATION or a waterfall (VALUES) or a penguin jumping headfirst off a glacier while other penguins watch (COURAGE—I hope the little guy aimed himself at water)? Well, those posters, despite the blurry connection between a waterfall and VALUES, were really, really popular in offices when they first came out. They brought a little bit of the wider world into what could be a depressing work space.

Your work space shouldn't need a labeled poster. What if the feeling people liked about those posters could simply be part of your décor? If your office could motivate you without you writing MOTIVATION across the wall or if it could inspire your sense of daring without the need to jump across a ravine? I want to help you create a space that motivates and inspires you without the need to stencil a giant picture of your favorite big jungle cat on the wall and write GO GET 'EM beneath it. (Fine, go with the big cat picture if you really want to, but I'm warning you it could be distracting . . . to put it gently.)

It can be hard deciding what décor can inspire you to do your best work. But despite how cliché they are, a hint can be found in those pictures I just mentioned. They are always of far-off places or extreme situations. They are meant to goad workers into achieving.

A well-designed room will inspire you, too. The more personal taste and effort that goes into decorating your office and building or altering the furnishings, the more continual proof you will have of what you're capable of. The best inspiration for me? Pictures of family. Reminders of why I am working my ass off to be the best I can be.

*CLUTTER IS THE KILLER OF A GREAT OFFICE DESIGN!

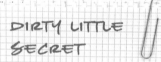
PRIVACY

Work requires a calm, stress-free environment. Some people think they can work anywhere, but the truth is you're always going to get more done when you have your own quiet space. This is why it is so great to have a home office—not only can you spend a normal workday in it, but if you have an hour or so in which you'd like to finish up some tasks, pay bills, or send some important e-mails, you'll do a better, faster job of it in an office setting than in a space geared toward utter relaxation or, even more tempting, entertainment.

If you have a studio apartment, small condo, or just want to partition a living room or den to add a home office, privacy screens are an excellent way to section the room. This is the idea behind cubicle offices. The difference is, however, that cubicle offices are horrible, whereas your personal space can be elegant in all ways, including the privacy walls. Lacking a wall, the best way to emphasize where the rest of a room stops and your office begins is through the use of privacy screens.

PRODUCTIVE LIGHTING

Home offices are slightly different in comparison to other rooms when it comes to lighting. Mood lighting is far less important than task lighting. But too much light feels sterile and harsh. You might be spending hours in your office, and no matter what you're doing you don't want to put any strain on your eyes due to lack of light. Make sure your entire space is properly lit with a combination of existing overhead lighting and directional task lighting.

TAKE CONTROL OF YOUR DESK

It's funny—desks are a piece of furniture that so many homes require, but there aren't many furniture vendors that will sell a good, stylish desk at a reasonable price. Don't get me wrong, there are some beauties to be had out there. The problem is you end up paying more for either fine wood or an antique finish. There is a huge lack of desks that are made better simply because of their shape and design. I have a suspicion that this is because there aren't many shapes better than a large flat surface with lots of leg room and (maybe) a few drawers. Also, desks

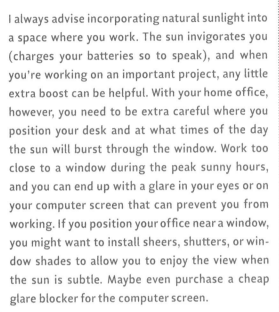

BEWARE THE GLARING DISTRACTION

I always advise incorporating natural sunlight into a space where you work. The sun invigorates you (charges your batteries so to speak), and when you're working on an important project, any little extra boost can be helpful. With your home office, however, you need to be extra careful where you position your desk and at what times of the day the sun will burst through the window. Work too close to a window during the peak sunny hours, and you can end up with a glare in your eyes or on your computer screen that can prevent you from working. If you position your office near a window, you might want to install sheers, shutters, or window shades to allow you to enjoy the view when the sun is subtle. Maybe even purchase a cheap glare blocker for the computer screen.

are assumed to be somewhat cluttered, unlike armoires, chairs, and other furniture that receive far more attention from designers. So if you're buying, you go big and get an antique or fine wood desk, or you keep cheap and end up with generic. You might have guessed this already. I'm not a fan of either.

Everyone wants and needs something different out of their desk: legroom on the right or the left; more drawers, fewer drawers, or no drawers; computer screen front and center or back and to the side; huge open space or just a few feet for drawing; only one spot to sit or the ability to approach it from all sides . . . the list goes on and on. Add color and material to that, and you've got an enormous range of preferences. Someone needs to address the poor selection out there. And it can be you!

My advice is to turn your desk modular. Buy the pieces of it separately and arrange them together to fit your specific needs. We buy our chairs separately from

Q.D.E. ALERT
ambiance

Your home office should have a calm, quiet, personal ambiance. You can control a lot of this with lighting and style of desk and accessories, but most importantly with the choice of where in the house to locate your office. The living room or an entertainment space is usually not the best call. An extra guest room, or an "empty nester's" second bedroom (formerly your college student's room) can work wonderfully, but you'll want to hide office supplies and electronics well so guests don't need to always be surrounded by the work environment while trying to rest. A basement can work well if you're sure to light it well and decorate it brightly if it's unfinished. Kitchens are highly popular for more than chefs. Many people are inspired in the kitchen and reminded of what they can do on the stove—fortunately cooking up a meal is not something you'll just do on a whim (turning on a TV, however, can happen all too quickly). Look for a space that has little physical distraction and is out of the way, but has enough space to accommodate everything you'll need for your office.

our desk—why not our drawers, shelves, colors, and finishes as well? After you buy different pieces, you can use a variety of paint, stencils, and other faux finishes (See the DIY Index, page 201) to bring all the separate parts of your desk together in style. Here are some tips on the best ways to combine separate pieces into your ideal desk.

Main surface

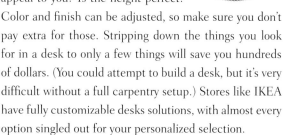

Find something with no fixtures attached. Size and appearance are what's important here. Do you like the thickness of the wood or the sheen of the metal? Do the legs appeal to you? Is the height perfect? Color and finish can be adjusted, so make sure you don't pay extra for those. Stripping down the things you look for in a desk to only a few things will save you hundreds of dollars. (You could attempt to build a desk, but it's very difficult without a full carpentry setup.) Stores like IKEA have fully customizable desks solutions, with almost every option singled out for your personalized selection.

Drawers

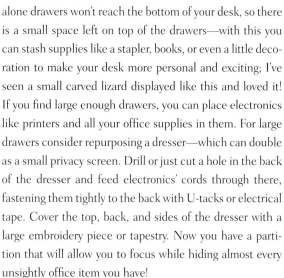

You need sizeable drawers for a desk, or make a file cabinet funky with personal accessories or cloth coverings. Small stand-alone drawers are all over the place and available in most design styles. Oftentimes stand-alone drawers won't reach the bottom of your desk, so there is a small space left on top of the drawers—with this you can stash supplies like a stapler, books, or even a little decoration to make your desk more personal and exciting; I've seen a small carved lizard displayed like this and loved it! If you find large enough drawers, you can place electronics like printers and all your office supplies in them. For large drawers consider repurposing a dresser—which can double as a small privacy screen. Drill or just cut a hole in the back of the dresser and feed electronics' cords through there, fastening them tightly to the back with U-tacks or electrical tape. Cover the top, back, and sides of the dresser with a large embroidery piece or tapestry. Now you have a partition that will allow you to focus while hiding almost every unsightly office item you have!

Shelves

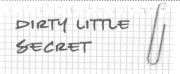

Hanging shelves on the wall is a great way to gain extra surface space and emphasize the office. Coloring and finishing of the shelves can pull together a sleek office look. If they're for pure office function, you'll want shelves that are deep enough to hold not just picture frames and décor but papers, folders, supplies, and whatever else you might keep there.

Chair

A chair that you'll spend so many hours in should be phenomenally comfortable. Try to find one that supports the lower back and is height adjustable. You'll want it to match the look of the space around it—but comfort comes first.

Alternatively, construct a desk from reclaimed materials; it's easier and far cheaper than you think!

Motivational Organization

A "To-Do" box and a "Done" box are great ways to see how much you're accomplishing. Not many things come in printed paper these days though, so you need something that can organize all sorts of notes and documents. My favorite and most customizable organization tool is also one of the easiest you'll ever make.

DIRTY LITTLE SECRET

LET YOUR WORK INSPIRE YOU

The office is one of the best spaces for DIY projects and your personal touch. Think about it: Would you rather work around some anonymous store-bought set of furniture or with something that was made with your own hands? Imagine having the undeniable evidence of the things you can achieve surrounding you as you work . . . it's a great way to throw self-doubt to the curb!

DIY
THE RECLAIMED COUNTRY-STYLE DESK

MATERIALS: three 2x4s, about eight pieces of 4" wide by 3' long pieces of reclaimed lumber or barn wood (search online for local wood recyclers), two 36"-high decorative stair banisters or table legs, wood glue, paint

TOOLS: drill, screws, chop saw or circular saw, paintbrush, level, measuring tape, stud finder

ASSEMBLY:

1. Create a U-shaped bracket out of 2x4s scaled to the width and length you want for your desk. Use wood glue, the drill, and screws to assemble the *U*.
2. Start screwing down your top planks of barn wood from the front working toward the back.
3. Attach your facing pieces on all three sides.
4. Mount a 2x4 that corresponds to the width of the desk surface as a cleat onto your wall at the appropriate height (matching the leg height). Drill the cleat into studs if you can find them with the stud finder (if not, use anchors).
5. Screw your legs onto the planked desk surface from the top down.
6. Attach the entire desk piece to the mounted cleat and screw it on through the top and side planks.
7. Sand and fill holes if needed (sealing with flat varnish is always a good alternative).

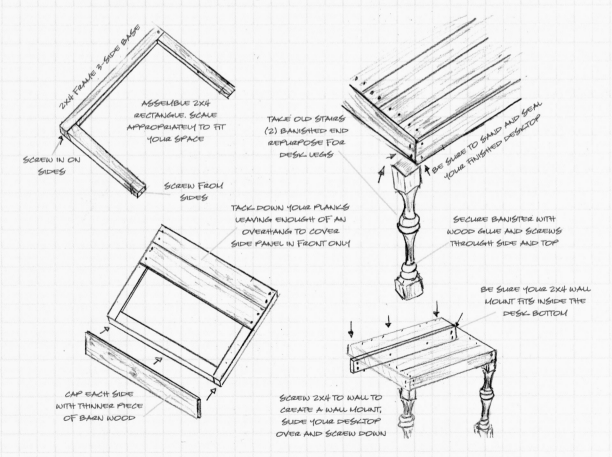

2X4 FRAME 3-SIDE BASE

ASSEMBLE 2X4 RECTANGLE. SCALE APPROPRIATELY TO FIT YOUR SPACE

SCREW IN ON SIDES

SCREW FROM SIDES

TAKE OLD STAIRS (2) BANISHED END REPURPOSE FOR DESK LEGS

BE SURE TO SAND AND SEAL YOUR FINISHED DESKTOP

TACK DOWN YOUR PLANKS LEAVING ENOUGH OF AN OVERHANG TO COVER SIDE PANEL IN FRONT ONLY

SECURE BANISTER WITH WOOD GLUE AND SCREWS THROUGH SIDE AND TOP

BE SURE YOUR 2X4 WALL MOUNT FITS INSIDE THE DESK BOTTOM

CAP EACH SIDE WITH THINNER PIECE OF BARN WOOD

SCREW 2X4 TO WALL TO CREATE A WALL MOUNT, SLIDE YOUR DESKTOP OVER AND SCREW DOWN

DIY
CUSTOMIZED CORKBOARD

MATERIALS: cheap framed mirror (plastic mirrors are very cheap, and you only need the frame), plain recycled corkboard, paint color of choice in two shades,

TOOLS: paintbrushes, pencil, spray-on industrial adhesive, box cutter or Exacto knife, stencil, clamps

ASSEMBLY:

1. Remove the mirror portion of the frame; with many products you can simply apply enough force to push it out.
2. Paint the corkboard the color of your choosing; one coat will usually do, but make it even.
3. Place the frame over the cork and trace the shape with a pencil. Cut around the pencil, leaving about a half inch of clearance to apply the adhesive.
4. Apply adhesive around the outer edge of the cork and fit the frame over it. Clamp at three points and let the board sit.
5. Now that the cork is in the frame, apply your stencil in the center—I like using a monogram in a darker shade than the painted cork.

PUTTING A LARGE FRAME
AROUND AN EXISTING
GROUP OF FRAMES
ADDS LAYERS OF STYLE
*

MY HOME OFFICE—
STYLISH, FUNCTIONAL, AND
FILLED WITH CREATIVE
INSPIRATION
*

DIY
MOLDING A BOOKSHELF

MATERIALS: bookshelf in need of a design change, beveled MDF molding, paint of choice, spray-on industrial adhesive

TOOLS: saw, paintbrushes, level

ASSEMBLY:

1. Measure the molding to fit each segment of the bookshelf and cut it with the saw.
2. Paint the molding in either the same color as the bookshelf or a color of your choosing for contrast.
3. Adhere the molding to the bookshelf with spray adhesive and a level.

WORK ON YOUR WALLS

There are some great and inexpensive products out there nowadays that can make surfaces writeable. These add lots of originality to your office design and are excellent ways to organize. If you have any cabinets or pullout drawers, consider replacing the fronts with glass or clear plastic. You can purchase some washboard markers and jot down notes and to-do lists all over your office! You can even do this with a glass or plastic desktop, and not only will you be surrounded by things you can't forget, but you're saving paper all the while. Check out your local hardware or paint store for some chalk paint. This stuff is great because you don't have to be afraid of writing an important note on a piece of paper or sticky note and losing it. If you jot all of your important information on your walls, you won't be able to miss it. Make sure you keep a box of chalk and an eraser handy nearby, possibly by mounting a low-profile wood tray like those in schools.

DIY
MAGNETIC PAINTED WALL WITH A FRAME

MATERIALS: large picture frame, magnetic paint

TOOLS: painter's tape, hammer, nails, paintbrush

ASSEMBLY:

1. Tape off an area on the wall in the same size and shape as the frame. Paint this with magnetic paint.
2. Remove the tape and hang the frame with nails.

GO GET 'EM!

Without a dedicated room, the home office is probably the hardest space to find a place for. Use my tips to make that easier and use the question "Will I be able to spend eight hours here at a time?" to be sure your choice of location is right. Once you find a space, use location and furnishings to separate it from the main space it is in—unless the room is a low-traffic area anyway. Customize your décor to inspire and focus you. Use modular and multipurpose furniture to combine storage, writing surfaces, style, and an ability to conceal office supplies when you want to take a break or call it a day. Light everything well to ease impact on your eyes as you work and allow this down-to-business space light up with your personal touch.

THE LOW-PROFILE PERMANENT OFFICE

One of my favorite things about separating a desk into modular parts is that you can make it seem more connected to your home. Shelves mounted to the wall instead of as freestanding furniture are a great example. It shows you really staked this area for yourself: no downsizing, no new office space, no nothing is going to change your office unless you say so! Unifying the furniture by color and finishing also provides an illusion that it was always there, almost part of the house itself. In this way, separating everything actually makes it feel more related.

PUTTING IT ALL TOGETHER
cohesion

Now you're ready to design a sanctuary for success that falls cohesively into your home's existing style. Imagine cutting your commute to zero minutes! The home office you build using my tips should allow you to surround yourself with things that motivate you and several places to turn that motivation into great, productive, and documented work. When the day ends, you should be able to hide almost everything away nicely and relax without being reminded of tomorrow's work. We have work to do every day of our lives—now you have your serene, personal place in which to do your best.

OPEN, CREATIVE, AND MULTIPLE
WORK SPACES MAKE THIS
HOME OFFICE SHINE. *

CHAPTER TEN

ENTERTAINING SPACES

Spaces for Parties, Dining, and Media Centers

It's easy to be lazy about gearing your home for entertaining. You might assume that if you have a living room, a television, and maybe some secondary seating, you are equipped to handle special occasions. But, my childhood memories have proven to me that that is not always the case. My mother was, and still is, a fantastic hostess. She was one of the biggest reasons my family was so close-knit. Entertaining was at the forefront of every minor and major occurrence in our lives. We not only hosted the standard get-togethers after cousin Joey's graduation or little Nicky's confirmation, but Mama also had a knack for bringing the neighbors in for coffee, snacks, games, and conversation almost daily. Here's how she pulled it off, as far as I can tell (one can never know all of Mom's ways, after all): Entertaining was never an inconvenience. She never had to scrounge for practical accommodations. Our guests could congregate in comfort in our living room for starters, but the overflow came quickly as Mama beckoned more people in. Fortunately, there were spaces ready to handle the hosting. The kitchen was always welcoming with seats at the counter and a rotating serving tray (which was almost like bait in a trap because Mom had a way of coaxing even the "toughest" of my buddies into helping to cook.) There was a window seat on the way out of the dining room that allowed people to sit and chat with those at the main table, which also stopped the conversations from intruding on the TV area, where yours truly loved to view his cartoons (they didn't have many home makeover shows back in the day, except for good old Bob Vila.) The whole house was filled with places for people to chat comfortably and facilitated a flow between these spots. Guests loved it. Also, my mother's fig cookies were out of this world.

TRUE CONFESSIONS

A guest on the show once asked me a favor. He grabbed my shoulder and said, "Frank, listen. I get that most of the home makeover shows build stuff that can be kind of flimsy, like a film set. Please just promise me one thing. If you can make any part of the new room solid, make it the area where I host a party. It doesn't even need to last much longer than the first time—please just make sure nothing breaks on the night I try to show off my famous new bar."

I laughed and told him not to worry; all of our work would be the real thing. Not just good-looking from afar, but durable stuff of which you can kick the tires. But I only told him this to distract him while I signaled an intern to hide the papier-mâché barstool he was carrying. (Just kidding!) He may have been wrong about our policy, but he was dead-on about where he would hang out with his friends. I truly believe that *your* absolute favorite part of your environment should be a private place that gives you escape and peace, but it's the entertainment space that guests often remember most. Because it is where they spend most of their time, this spot will form the core of the impression others will have of your home. But these tips will help your place of hosting make an even greater impression on your guests. A major characteristic of a space for hosting is that it can happen anywhere. There are near-limitless possibilities as to where in your house, or even within a given room, you will choose to situate the spot to settle down with visitors. Let's think about where the best place to entertain is in *your* home. First, let's go over the rooms in which you definitely won't be telling people to "relax and get comfortable." Then we'll talk about the best rooms in which to set up an entertainment space.

Q.D.E. ALERT
function

What follows are some of my favorite tips, tricks, and techniques to help you design the ultimate series of spaces in which your guests can socialize. We're also going to provide them points of interest that may act as conversation pieces to socialize around. The overall idea is to have vignettes for socializing that work together in a network so guests can mill and travel around your home and always feel welcome and open to converse.

DON'TS AND DOS

Don't:

* The bedroom. The most important of the private rooms, this is the opposite of a place to entertain guests except in circumstances that I don't need to discuss here.
* The bathroom. Or maybe this is the most important private room . . . either way, this ain't no place for entertaining. Not that a few magazines aren't nice.
* Entryways. These are definitely part of your guests' experience, but if your entryway is large enough for a group to spend time in it, you might want to consider converting part of it to a living area. Also, a good rule of thumb for entertainment areas is to avoid too much traffic through them ("Hey, quit blocking the TV!").

Do:

* The living room: What this really means is sectioning out a space from your existing living room and dedicating it to entertaining. The thing to keep an eye on here is balance—especially with features like TVs, game fixtures, and bars. You want the main living room to be separate so everyone present doesn't need to focus on the entertainment center. However, you also want to be able to combine all your seating for those occasions when you do host a large group.
* The dining room: No question, this will be your largest entertainment vignette without a television, so focus on seating and upscale décor.
* The kitchen: Neglecting a place for guests in the kitchen is a very bad idea! If your friends can't be present while you cook you miss out on chatting, showing off, and (most important of all) help.
* The dedicated entertainment room: So you've cleared out a whole room that is for fun only? Great! Entertainment is often the first thing people think of when they have an extra room, and I totally agree!

A COMMON PROBLEM: THE ELEPHANT IN THE ROOM

The television. These days, when people talk about entertainment spaces, it seems as if they instantly think of TVs, video games, and other electronic toys. You might have

even thought this chapter was totally dedicated to media centers. It's not. Popular TV shows add to the media craze by constantly featuring the lavish home theaters, elaborate game rooms, and plush lounge spaces of the rich and famous. Lacking a rock-star budget, make sure you only spend as much on these things as you need to enjoy them. The other upgrades—and there will always be upgrades—are just status symbols. Besides, the style of your space as a whole is a much better symbol of yourself. Most of the entertaining space trends you see today mix personal style and technology into visual and audio-driven environments geared toward the modern tech-savvy family. As a designer, these types of spaces are fun and really easy to create because of the direct focus on the media center. The most challenging and most rewarding projects, however, offer the option of multimedia fun without making it the constant center of attention. Who the heck has the time or the money to keep up with the expensive and advanced state-of-the-art equipment it takes to outfit the ultimate entertaining space, anyway? I'm calling for a return to the basics. Focus on creating a place to spend time with the people you share your life with now, and make it a room for new people who you want to invite into your world.

HIDING THE TV

Masking the TV so that it's not the first thing your guests notice when they enter the space is a foolproof way to make the space more social. Closed-storage media units are a great way to tuck away the old-style TVs (anything that's not a flat screen). The downside is that store-bought units can be expensive and clunky (though cheaper versions come out all the time). The other downside to those really into style is that often media units are so obvious that it's not all that much better than just letting the TV hang out. There are plenty of more creative and less obvious ways to stow the set. But if you have a flat screen hung on a wall, the challenge of hiding it just increased tenfold!

On one episode of *Design on a Dime,* I cut the back out of a decorative medicine cabinet and hung it over the screen. Flea markets are full of classic as well as surprising options; often all you need is a saw and a few screws. Make sure you have at least two inches of clearance between the TV screen and the closed cabinet door.

There are plenty of more exotic ways to disguise it, like an armoire or a privacy screen (again, keep your eyes peeled in the thrift markets). If you have a flat-screen TV, try using large-scale artwork or a mirror as a cover.

The placement of your TV and media center typically depends on the layout, architecture, and electrical plan of your room. But you don't have to be a slave to the fixed elements in your floor plan. Cord covers can be purchased at most hardware stores and are a great, inexpensive way to hide unsightly wires. This will give you more freedom to allow your personal taste to determine where the TV goes, not the electrician. At last, freedom from dangling cords!

TAKE CONTROL OF YOUR LIGHTING

Controllable lighting makes your entertainment space much more variable. Picture a cocktail party lit by everyday bright overhead light, and then picture the same party under a dimmer glow. The dimmer is more relaxing and intimate; it confirms that the workday is over, and it actually encourages people to stand closer to each other.

Dimmer switches are the easiest way to control your existing lighting. They can be purchased at your local hardware store and are easy to install with a screwdriver. Here are a few other ways to control your lighting:

Mood Lighting
This consists of unfixed units that you will use instead of the room's main lighting when entertaining. There are so many options because designers love to create new lighting fixtures. There is plenty of variety to be found online without spending more than $25. The cheapest, most classic mood lighting? Candles.

New Installed Lighting
Look for fixtures like wall sconces, up lights, and directional lighting that can be pointed at specific features in your space. If you have artwork or movie posters, a directional light aimed at either provides a gallery feel.

Natural Light
If you're lucky enough to have a home that is filled with windows that let in a lot of natural light, consider purchasing dark, thick curtains so you don't have to wait until nightfall to screen your favorite flick.

Q.D.E. ALERT
ambiance

Reducing the brightness of a room is the most effective way to send the message that it's time to relax. Especially when hosting a large group at night, lowering the light signals that the party has started.

DIY
THE SLEEK MODERN BAR

MATERIALS: five 6' long 2x4s, two sheets of ¾" 4x8 MDF, five pieces of reclaimed Plexiglas (cut at a hardware store or glass cutter to be about 4' high, length depending on your room's dimensions), 1" steel washers, about ten pieces of 18" tile (try to find old or discontinued tile from discount stores), two LED strip lights (optional)

TOOLS: screws and wood screws, circular saw, handsaw or chop saw, drill, wood glue, tile adhesive, jigsaw

ASSEMBLY:

1. Using 2x4s, wood screws, and wood glue, create a basic two-tier frame about 4' long by 2½' deep (size and scale will vary based on your room size; cut the 2x4s down where needed).
2. Cut ¾" MDF to fit over the top surface of the frame (better yet, have Home Depot cut it for you).
3. Using your jigsaw, cut down and notch out corners of MDF shelves to fit snugly around the 2x4 frame pieces.
4. Use your reclaimed Plexiglas to face the front and sides of the bar frame. Be sure to carefully pre-drill holes where you want to screw the Plexiglas onto the bar frame. (Cutting Plexiglas isn't easy, so be sure to consult local glass shops for help.)
5. Use 1" washers and steel screws to secure the Plexiglas and create a decorative look.
6. Glue your tiles to the top surface of the bar.
7. (Optional) For a glowing effect, add LED strip lights to the inside of the bar.

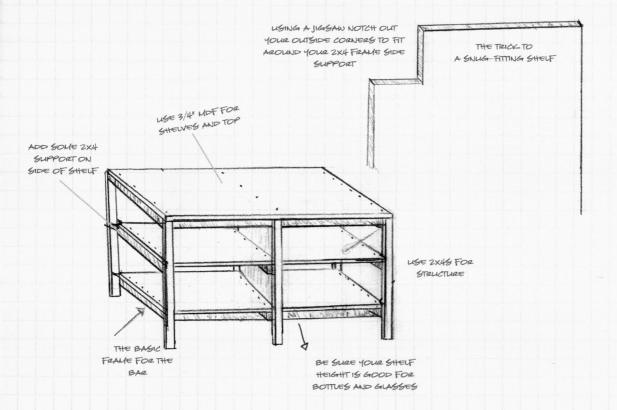

USING A JIGSAW NOTCH OUT YOUR OUTSIDE CORNERS TO FIT AROUND YOUR 2X4 FRAME SIDE SUPPORT

THE TRICK TO A SNUG-FITTING SHELF

USE 3/4" MDF FOR SHELVES AND TOP

ADD SOME 2X4 SUPPORT ON SIDE OF SHELF

USE 2X4S FOR STRUCTURE

THE BASIC FRAME FOR THE BAR

BE SURE YOUR SHELF HEIGHT IS GOOD FOR BOTTLES AND GLASSES

SUPERNATURAL LIGHTING

Himalayan rock salt lamps are a stunning way to add ambiance and energy to a space. Made of natural stones that vary from shades of pink and peach to fiery oranges, they provide soothing light and uncommon color. Rock salt is well known for its therapeutic effects and is also a natural air purifier. It's also a definite conversation piece. Prices usually start around $30.

HIGH-STYLE LIGHTING SOLUTIONS RANKED BY ESTIMATED CHEAPNESS

1. Candles

2. Dimmers

3. Mood lighting

4. Natural rock salt lamp

THE BAR

The ability to mix a classy beverage is the hallmark of a great host. Many great hosts, however, lack a bar to mix behind. Ranging from an attractive console for storing bottles to all-out lacquered mahogany, I've built bars to fit rooms of all sizes and styles. No matter what sort of space you have to work with and how noticeable you want the bar to be when not in use, I have three versions that are easy to adjust depending on what materials you can find and purchase.

THE KITCHEN ENTERTAINMENT SPACE

It may seem that seating is the most important element to entertaining company in the kitchen. It depends, however, on where your guests plop themselves down. A table placed away from the main cooking area or at a lower height than the kitchen counter(s) places an unneeded obstacle between the chef and the guests. A counter space where the guests can sit and converse with whoever is cooking is ideal, but we don't want guests to feel they are in the way. A counter dedicated to serving, instead of cooking, is a great focal point for an entertainment space located in the kitchen. Use this as a staging ground for hors d'ouevres or mixing drinks. Be sure to include tall seating.

DIY
THE TUCK-AWAY MOBILE BAR

MATERIALS: any small multi-tiered wheeled metal table, two or more pieces of 1x2 wood in the same length as the table, two pieces of bead board in height and length of table's short sides, one bead board in height and length of table's long side, black paint or dark stain, wood fill

TOOLS: drill, screws, wood glue

ASSEMBLY:

1. Purchase a multi-tiered wheeled rack from any inexpensive home goods or department store. Wood or metal top both work, but wood is preferable.

2. Paint or stain the top surface of the table if it is wood. Arrange the bead board on the short sides by first drilling holes through the bead board into the side of the tabletop then drilling screws in.

3. Use wood glue to arrange the 1x2 wood on the inner shelf so that bottles can be organized in rows. Allow the glue to set.

4. Adhere the long bead board along one of the long sides using the same drill method as before. Fill the holes with wood fill and paint or stain.

YOUR THEME FOR FUN

The two classic entertainment room themes are movies and sports. Most of the DIY projects you'll find in this section use one of those two as inspiration, but you should feel free to replace those with anything you like! Just think about your favorite hobby and what colors, objects, and artwork capture the essence of that thing that gives you joy. Many of these projects will easily adapt to fit your hobby if you simply substitute the central item for something you love.

THE DINING ROOM ENTERTAINMENT SPACE

You're going to orient your dining room around your table, which is a good call. That doesn't need to be it, though. Plenty of dining rooms are only used for dining, which is a waste of high-quality space. Carry the idea of entertainment vignettes into the dining room, and orient them around the table so that smaller groups feel welcome at less formal occasions than only sitting down to dinner. Side seating with more than one chair, or a soft lighting fixture, will lure guests into lingering in your dining room even when there is no food.

THE DEDICATED ENTERTAINMENT SPACE

So far I've only talked about how to hide the multimedia. There is the possibility, though, that the higher-tech entertainment items have their own rooms. It's also possible that, already having splurged on your electronics, you are left with only enough money to put a few cushions on the floor and pretend to be blind to the sad, starkly decorated room around the TV screen. But it doesn't have to be that way! Entertainment spaces are always a blast for decorators, because we can be creative in capturing our clients' personalities in ways that aren't really possible in other rooms. Both on the show and throughout my years as a professional decorator I learned how to use the last little bits of a budget to assemble truly awesome spaces dedicated to fun. The key is to use inexpensive materials to focus attention on interesting items that express how *you* like to have fun!

DIY
SHADOW BOX DISPLAY CASE

MATERIALS: shallow dresser drawers, black paint

TOOLS: screwdriver, paintbrush, level, small black nails, hammer, handsaw

ASSEMBLY:

1. Remove all knobs from the dresser drawers with a screwdriver.
2. Paint the inside of the drawers and, depending on how you like the look, the outside as well. If the bottom of a drawer's faceplate extends past the bottom of the drawer, saw off the excess so that the drawer will sit flush against the wall.
3. After the paint dries, use the level to position the drawers against the wall with the wider front portion facing the floor. Nail the drawers to the wall with two to four small nails.
4. Place items for display on your new shadow boxes!

DIY
WILD SKATEBOARD PICTURE FRAME

MATERIALS: old skateboard or cheap new one, black and white semi-gloss paint, heavy stock clear transparency paper, three photos of choice, flat thumbtacks, picture-hanging kit

TOOLS: drill, paint brush, jigsaw, sandpaper, hammer, measuring tape

ASSEMBLY:

1. Start by removing any hardware from the board (wheels, etc).
2. Fill and sand any holes.
3. Measure out three rectangles slightly smaller than the photos' size and evenly spaced down the board vertically. Mark these with a pencil.
4. Using a jigsaw, cut the squares.
5. Sand all edges and paint your base color white.
6. Create simple zebra stripes with black gloss paint.
7. Cut transparency paper down to picture size and sandwich two pieces around a picture.
8. Using a thumbtack, mount each photo to the skateboard from the rear.

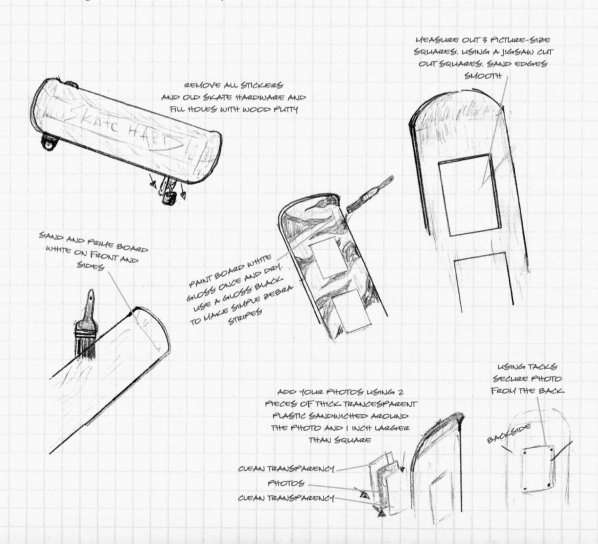

REMOVE ALL STICKERS AND OLD SKATE HARDWARE AND FILL HOLES WITH WOOD PUTTY

MEASURE OUT 3 PICTURE-SIZE SQUARES. USING A JIGSAW CUT OUT SQUARES. SAND EDGES SMOOTH

SAND AND PRIME BOARD WHITE ON FRONT AND SIDES

PAINT BOARD WHITE GLOSS ONCE AND DRY. USE A GLOSS BLACK TO MAKE SIMPLE ZEBRA STRIPES

ADD YOUR PHOTOS USING 2 PIECES OF THICK TRANCESPARENT PLASTIC SANDWICHED AROUND THE PHOTO AND 1 INCH LARGER THAN SQUARE

USING TACKS SECURE PHOTO FROM THE BACK

BACKSIDE

CLEAN TRANSPARENCY
PHOTOS
CLEAN TRANSPARENCY

The Home Theater You
Never Thought Possible

A real cinema contains more than just a big silver screen. There's the lobby with all of its posters, the candy counter, and not to mention the big dark room that lets you watch the screen in the best environment possible. In a home theater, re-creating these extras is the key to success. One of my most rewarding projects on the show re-created this experience in a small space for a fraction of the usual cost of home theaters. *And now, our main attraction:* the super low-budget home movie theater!

The Entryway

A movie theater is one of the few places where candy passes for décor. Use the instructions in this chapter to build a custom display case, or do what I did on the show: find an old jewelry display case in a flea market, faux finish the metal to look like wood, and place it at the entry filled with traditional theater treats! On the wall behind the counter I propped some old film art and trinkets to drive home the theme. If you can't find a standing display case, any wall-mounted storage solution can work as long as it's open (not a cabinet). The same treatments will work.

DIY
THE CANDY COUNTER

MATERIALS: table or old glass display case, vintage candy signs, candy in packages, velvet (optional)

TOOLS: staple gun (optional)

ASSEMBLY:

This is more of a scavenging-type DIY. Look for restaurant supply stores and online retailers who supply signs for various iconic candy brands. Old commercial display cases can be found at flea markets—a good cleaning will fix one up. Alternatively, simply upholster a small table with dark velvet (stapling the velvet to the underside) and display your candy there.

Make a Mock Lobby

This is an excellent place to use furniture and objects that you love, but for which you haven't yet found a place. For the lobby of the home theater I built on the show, we placed a café-style table for four. I hung a magazine rack on the wall behind the table, and I recommend doing something similar because posters aren't the only way to recall your favorite movies and stars. Seek out those classic cover shots!

The Screen

Position your TV and other media at the center of whichever wall will allow you to stand as far as possible from the screen. This creates more length in the zone and a pronounced focal point for the theater.

The Audience

Place your primary seating at a comfortable watching distance. If the height of the TV screen allows, place secondary seating in a row behind the couch. Use a semicircle pattern to reduce the width of the overall seating area. Narrowness is important here.

The Curtains

Surprisingly, curtains are the most important money-saving part of your home theater. You might have thought they were a total luxury. Find a large, dark curtain—or series of them—in either velvet or something cheaper that reminds you of the movies. Follow my hanging instructions, which will allow for adjustments to fit whatever space you have. Just think of it as an extended version of putting up normal window curtains.

Now we have work to do in the room outside the curtain. Sound insulation is a great idea that can bring style along with it. Because a home theater is something you will want to add to in the future, this step might be useful even if you don't have high-powered speakers yet. You want to install the sound insulation along a long wall and, if you have a choice, the wall that is closest to the rest of the house.

Movie theaters also typically have some architectural flair that recalls the early gilded age of Hollywood. For my theater on *Design on a Dime*, I made custom display walls for posters. They really topped off the feeling of escaping to the movies. The best part is that if you faux it, you can create this dramatic feel of architecture for less than $100.

There you have it: the ability to totally escape into the world of movies! All inexpensive and all made with your own two hands.

DIY
SNAZZY SOUND INSULATING

MATERIALS: 1'-square pieces of ¼" MDF (enough to cover wall to be insulated), cotton batting, faux leather in two colors cut in 1½' squares

TOOLS: staple gun, industrial mirror-hanging adhesive, level

ASSEMBLY:

1. Upholster all the MDF squares, an equal number in each color fabric, by spraying adhesive on them, sticking lots of cotton batting on, and stapling the fabric to the back of the MDF.
2. Arrange the squares in a geometric pattern: vertical strips, horizontal stripes, or diagonal like a chessboard. Use a level and pencil to make sure they are all straight.
3. Adhere all the squares to the wall with industrial adhesive.

DIY
CLASSIC CINEMA WALLS WITH BLACK-AND-WHITE POSTERS

MATERIALS: MDF molding, metallic paint, latex paint, poster frame, movie poster

TOOLS: painter's tape, paintbrush, roller, finishing nails, wood glue, hand-or chop saw, hammer, wood fill, nails for hanging

ASSEMBLY:

1. Paint your molding with your desired color of metallic paint. Tape off a rectangular section of the wall—wider and much taller than your poster frames—and paint that area with your latex color.
2. When the paint dries, remove the tape and hang the molding with wood glue and finishing nails. Fill nail holes with wood fill and metallic paint.
3. Place the posters in the poster frames in the middle of the molding rectangle.
4. Repeat for a series of poster vignettes.

DIY
360-DEGREE CURTAIN ENCLOSURE

MATERIALS: five or six (depending on length) curtains in fabric of choice, five or six long curtain rods

TOOLS: drill, screws, ladder

ASSEMBLY:

1. The length and number of curtains and rods you need will depend greatly on your space. Leave at least 4' between the television and the first seats, but feel free to close the curtain enclosure right behind the farthest seat. Keep the width as narrow as seating permits.
2. Once your dimensions are figured out, simply hang the curtain rods from your ceiling with a drill and screws: Position them so that the curtains fully enclose the screening and seating area (if possible). Creating three sides of a rectangle with curtains—the screen against a wall forming the fourth side—works well.

GO GET 'EM!

With the advice in this chapter you should be able to set up a series of spots, in addition to your main entertaining space, that will allow a gathering to grow, move, and socialize as it should. You're also now equipped to decorate your own entertainment center.

PUTTING IT ALL TOGETHER
cohesion

Every entertainment space should contain seating where people can get comfortable, an object of interest to gather around that is not necessarily a TV, and ambient features that signal it's time to relax and socialize. To facilitate the flow of a party between spaces, consider unifying themes of color or objects between several entertainment spaces in different rooms. Thinking about what types of conversations your guests will be having in different entertainment spaces can help guide your design. If this was someone else's home and you were among the first guests at a party, would you know where to socialize?

CHAPTER ELEVEN

OUTDOOR SPACES

Add a Room to Your Home—No Walls Needed

Ah yes, the great outdoors. It can seem like a wild, untamable place. Certainly it's the domain of a landscaping artist more than an interior decorator like yours truly. Well, call me stubborn, but I've made it a habit to bring my design method outside . . . and it's worked! With only a few changes of materials, I've found that you can treat outdoor spaces the way you would rooms with four walls. In fact, doing so adds a stylish contrast of raw nature with suave décor. So my advice is to treat your outdoor space like an indoor one and then take advantage of the unique items you can use outside that aren't possible inside. The outdoor space I designed for the Chicago Merchandise Mart's "Dream Home" is one of my favorites.

Of course, before you jump into an outside design, the climate and seasonality of where you live will dictate the amount of time you will spend outside *and* the materials you use in your building projects. The sad truth is that if you only have half a year of good outdoor weather, then you should probably only spend half the money as someone with beautiful weather all year round. The sunny side of that is how much we can do for your outdoor space with even a small budget. Don't forget that six months is a long, happy time when you can sit comfortably in the fresh air and sun for most of it!

TRUE CONFESSIONS

Let me tell you of the great storm of *Design on a Dime*. We were working with a house whose owners wanted it transformed into a Tuscan villa. My pride and joy, which was sure to become the owner's pride and joy, was a beautiful textured plaster wall with a rounded red stone top that would form the longest border of the backyard. With a simple plywood skeleton and plenty of elbow grease behind the plastering trowel, the fence easily fit into our $1,000 budget for the entire project. I'm tearing up as I write this, and it's not even because of the sheer beauty of that fence. It's because we had to build it twice.

On the second day of filming we were 90 percent finished with the final layer of plaster. A flash storm hit. As soon as the rain began falling I started dashing around looking for whatever tarp I could find. We were able to cover the first five feet of the plaster, but I watched the rest of the fence melt in the driving rain. It was a disaster. I'd seen plenty of on-site setbacks throughout my career and was

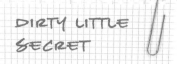

TAKE THE INSIDE OUT

Look at your exterior space and design it with the same principles with which you approach interior rooms. Treat the environment as your own décor—it can help dictate color, texture, and scale. With this perspective, the more rugged materials needed for outdoor furnishing will fall purposefully in with your design plan.

skilled at rolling with the punches, but when the fence turned to mush I couldn't so much as look at a camera.

In the end the network recouped our loss, chalking it up as an "act of God" (the money made me feel better but the reason was a bit of a blow). We rebuilt the fence with a full-on party tent over it—needless to say, it was sunny for the rest of the shoot. The moral of this story: Know the weather when doing delicate work outdoors and have protection like tarps or an open garage available for quick cover. If you can learn from that tragedy, it will make me feel a little better about it.

Q.D.E. ALERT
function

The function of your outdoor space's design should be to facilitate the same ease and comfort as the coziest place inside your home. You will also be able to add features that cannot exist inside. If you think of an outdoor space as a room equal in status to your living room, you'll automatically start to come up with ways to ease the transition between inside and out. If you can design a space that, on a nice day, makes the door between indoors and out seem as minor to use as a door between a kitchen and living room, then you've designed a successful outdoor space.

DON'TS AND DOS

Don't:

* Treat your outdoor space as if it will automatically be less comfortable than your indoor space.
* Think that a lack of temperate weather year-round means it's not worth designing a wonderful outdoor space.
* Underestimate flower gardens as anything less than the most satisfying décor there is.
* Think an urban outdoor space is not worth decorating.

Do:

* Carry indoor design techniques to your outdoor project.
* Install some manner of outdoor shelter—even the cheapest will serve you for several seasons.
* Envision your outdoor space as a series of comfortable and functional zones.
* Make the most of possibilities like fire and water that are rarely possible indoors.

A COMMON PROBLEM: WHAT TO DO, WHAT TO DO

With outdoor space, more is better. There is no good reason to want less space to work with. Yet some people can be overwhelmed by the size of a porch, balcony, yard, or patio and simply choose to plop a grill down and call it a day. A better way to approach open spaces is to create zones, just like you would with social spaces indoors. Think first about what outdoor-only features you definitely want, such as a fire pit, a screened-in area, a walkway or patio, a fountain, a pool, or—if you have enough space—a spot for lawn games like horseshoes and bocce. Essentially anything that you've placed in your outdoor space can be a center that you position seating and décor vignettes around. After those focal centers are determined, go about decorating and positioning as you would indoors. Don't be afraid to combine several seating and table vignettes into a larger social cluster.

Design an outdoor space that allows you to entertain, spend time with family, cook, and hang with friends just as you do inside. Merging the outdoors and the indoors through great design is an easy way to expand your overall living area. Of course, there are different challenges to outdoor home design, such as how to keep the dirt out and means of adequate light at night. But technology has merged with outdoor design to provide you with fine furniture lines, lighting fixtures, and rugged mimics of popular indoor textiles. I have even seen flat-screen TVs built into outdoor spaces!

When choosing colors and textures, work with the natural environment to bring cohesion and balance to your outdoor space. Your design plan should utilize and enhance the outer architecture of your house and the look of the region. Remember to work with the surroundings and not against them. Nature is beautiful in itself, so try to incorporate plants and flowers and bring color into your designs.

OUTDOOR MATERIALS

Changing the materials you use will change the way your outdoor space looks even if you bring an interior design philosophy. Use this to your advantage. Some durable materials bring major style points if you expand the extent that you use them past what's traditional. Bead board is a material used almost exclusively for wainscoting, but it's also relatively inexpensive. My friend used bead board for all four walls of his porch *and* the ceiling, and the effect was phenomenal!

DIRTY LITTLE SECRET

OUTDOOR BLUEPRINTS ARE POSSIBLE

Having trouble envisioning your outdoor zones? Try using rope, tape, washable outdoor spray paint, or sticks to lay out squares that will help you envision how your zones will fit and come together.

The lesson here is to embrace unique outdoor materials in an indoor way. Even if it's for new construction, you'll often save money by not needing insulation and using a low-demand material.

THE BEST OUTDOOR VIGNETTES

Following are some unique items and projects for an outdoor space. I'll provide ideas for types of seating and décor that you can base a whole sitting area around. Like in a living room, you should focus on arranging seating vignettes so that the comfort of an indoor home is carried outside.

Lighting

Just like in a well-designed interior, all your effort can be for nothing without proper lighting. While during the day you can utilize natural sunlight, when it gets dark you must have sufficient fixtures ready. Make sure to add

GREAT MATERIALS FOR THE GREAT OUTDOORS

* Pressure-treated woods (plywood or 2x4s)
* All weather-resistant stains
* Synthetic plastics
* Bead board
* Repurposed wood and metal

Q.D.E. ALERT
ambiance

Nature will provide most of the ambiance in your outdoor space. Bringing interior vibes and creature comforts will complete the feeling by adding contrast. Try embracing materials that say something about your surroundings: Use wood and found objects from the area. Use rugged outdoor materials for indoor-type purposes. Chairs with ottomans, rugs, and side tables for drinks can all find a spot in your outdoor space alongside plants, firelight, and the wider world. Playing up the contrast lends a totally unique ambiance to outdoor spaces.

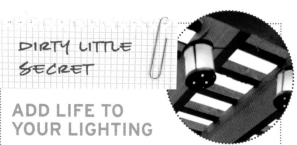
ADD LIFE TO YOUR LIGHTING

To emphasize the tie between your décor and the natural world, try combining your lighting with plants. A potted plant with white Christmas lights strung around it or an electric lantern sitting in the soil next to a plant are wonderful items to base a vignette around.

ground-level lighting to all walkways and paths, similar to the lighting you see along movie theater aisles when the lights go out. Be sure to check out the variety of stylish choices available. More stylized outdoor lighting includes torches, fireplaces, candles, floodlights, and hanging lanterns. Fireplaces, citronella candles, and certain tiki torches do wonders in repelling insects.

In my opinion, flame and lanterns are the two essential outdoor lighting solutions. Tiki torches are great if you're working on a seating vignette in an area without hard floors. For patios and porches, start with strings of lanterns along the edges of the roof or in nearby trees. Chinese-style paper lanterns offer lots of opportunity for style. Try purchasing plain white lanterns and using a stencil to add a unique, personal pattern to them. White Christmas tree lights can also be strung up to make a starry effect even on overcast nights.

Chain-Suspended Platform Bed

This project will really impress company but is not very hard at all. The idea is to suspend a wood platform from the ceiling of a porch and make a lounging bed out of it. The contrast of metal chains and wood against luxurious pillows and blankets is a prime example of the unique decorating opportunities available when you bring an indoor philosophy outside. One trip to the hardware store will get you the wood and chains you need, then use extra pillows and blankets to complete the look.

Rugged Rugs

On a porch, patio, or pool deck where the floor is totally uniform, adding a rug can both vary things up and anchor a nice seating area. Durable rugs for outdoor spaces are cheaper than indoor rugs. Choose from the following options, and center some chairs around your exciting new outdoor rug. It will seem like you had a gorgeous living room, then knocked the four walls down to let in the sun.

* Rugs made of synthetic fibers like polypropylene can be both weatherproof and surprisingly soft.
* Mats decorated with colors and patterns that mimic vibrant Persian rugs are a bold statement that you've brought all your style out from inside.
* Bamboo rugs are made of one of the most sustainable materials on the planet. They can be found in raw, natural looks or dyed and spun to look like a textile rug.

DIRTY LITTLE SECRET

YOU WON'T REGRET IT

In Hawaii, most houses are built standard with a lanai, an open-air patio. It's not surprising that everyone who lives in Hawaii has an outdoor space that is just as essential as their other rooms. I would say it's surprising that Americans everywhere don't crave outdoor spaces as much as an indoor living room. None of this country is in a region that never has great weather. No matter where you live, take a pointer from the peaceful energy of the islands and create a roof-covered outdoor place to wind down and catch a breath of fresh air. If you think you can't afford it, remember that if you treat it like a new indoor room then it really will be a bargain.

OUTDOOR FABRICS: NOT SO DIFFERENT AFTER ALL!

Not everything outdoors has to be hard wood or metal. Don't be afraid to use fabric! There are lots of great all-weather fabrics out there that are durable for the outdoors, but if you really want luxury, try indoor fabrics that you simply take inside with you. Employing soft pillows and blankets that you can bring inside at night will make your outdoor living area more inviting. Try leaving these items in a basket by the door as an invitation to casually wander outside to relax.

Fire

Another great thing about outdoor space is that you can incorporate elements you might not be able to use in your interior space. Fire is an exemplary design element to introduce into an outdoor space. Add a fire pit, a built-in fireplace, or, if you don't have the room, standing torches. Layer your space with candles and hang pre-lit pendant lamps from your trees. Hanging firelight creates a fantastic nighttime ambiance. Fireplaces will extend the season for outdoor living as a heat source and gathering point. And who doesn't love s'mores?

One fireplace solution is the 360-degree fire pit. If you aren't on a hard surface, simply dig a hole that's a few inches deep and around 4 feet in diameter, then encircle that with stones. If you have a stone or brick patio, finding a metal fire bowl—often copper—is a classy solution that fits just about every design style. If you want a smaller fire, try a charcoal hibachi grill. Even if you don't cook on it, the glow of coals in a hibachi are a calming, subdued way to bring the presence of flame to your outdoor space without a full blaze.

Small-Scale Gardening

Potted plants and flower boxes liven up an outdoor space. Integrating the pot or flower box into your design style will emphasize the harmony of your design with nature. Plants, like well-executed design, will serve as a daily testament of your expert touch in your home.

GO GET 'EM!

Once you have created an outdoor space that connects seamlessly with the rest of your home, you'll truly be able to appreciate nature on a daily basis. Even with a small urban nest, you can employ my methods to create an inviting vignette that will beckon you out for some much-needed fresh air. Remember the goals of bringing your indoor design methods outside and reflecting the ambiance of the natural surroundings with your décor. Play up that contrast between indoor function and outdoor style. Don't think each vignette you design in your room without walls needs to be laid out differently than the vignettes in your living room. Enjoy the beautiful weather in your new outdoor room!

DIRTY LITTLE SECRET

FAKE YOUR FLOWER BOX

More elaborate design styles will run the cost of a simple wooden flower box far higher than it needs to be. This is a perfect opportunity to get creative with wood graining and stenciling (see page 13). Using bright colors can add a more welcoming, eclectic cabin feel. Painting a simple wood box black and using a metallic paint like silver or gold for stenciling will yield a more urban or modern look.

PUTTING IT ALL TOGETHER
cohesion

Lit by day with sunlight and by night with glowing lamps and flickering firelight, you'll love your new outdoor space. Bring soft blankets and pillows from inside out to soften the durable materials that you leave outside. Consider the numerous new ways to bring intricate indoor design outside without betraying the look of your regional nature. Lay out the items in your outdoor space the same way you would lay them out in a living room. Finally, embrace the unique benefits of an outdoor space like fireplaces, flowing water, and gardening.

RESOURCES

FRANK'S FAVES

Here's a list of some of my favorite sites that I support, create, and work with!

www.dirtylittlesecretsofdesign.com
Catch behind-the-scenes video and photos of the making of this book.

www.frankfontana.net
My official Web site.

www.twitter.com/frankfontana
My official Twitter page.

www.hgtv.com
A great resource for everything home and garden from the network that started it all.

www.todayshow.com
My good buddies and my home away from home.

www.mudd360.com
An awesome ad agency and digital company that helps me with my projects.

www.jabrealestate.com
Great real-estate development group out of Chicago that I design buildings and model units for; I also shot some great photos of their office "mancave."

www.beprimitive.com
A multi-level cultural mecca located in the heart of downtown Chicago that offers a wide selection of imported, handcrafted home goods. Also one of our favorite shoot locations!

www.kennethludwig.com
My man with the floor plan, Ken's showroom at the Merchandise Mart is my playground for shopping in high style for a reasonable cost. If you like Z Gallerie, Pottery Barn, and CB2 then you will love Ken!

www.goodwill.org
If you paid attention the earlier chapters you will remember my eco conscious 3 R's method (refurbish, recycle, repaint) and on my show, you've heard me mention Goodwill as my source for shopping, whether I'm looking for a vintage wooden file cabinet or a destination for finding items when redecorating a place. But what you probably don't know is that in its more than 100 years of existence, Goodwill has been an entrepreneurial leader, environmental pioneer and social innovator of the "reduce, reuse, recycle" practice.

Goodwill sells donated clothing in its thousands of retail stores across the country and in Canada, as well as online at shopgoodwill.com, the first and only nonprofit Internet auction site.

Revenue raised through the sale of usable clothing and other goods funds Goodwill's important social services and transforms the simple act of cleaning out a closet into environmental stewardship. The revenue is used to fund job-training programs, employment placement services, and other important community-based services that benefit millions of people each year.

SUPPLIES, INNOVATORS, AND TOOLS

www.homedepot.com
Pretty obvious. They have it all when it comes to home-improvement DIY tools, materials, etc. Try walking down aisles that you wouldn't typically walk down to find some unique materials that might be purposed for one project, but that can be repurposed for your art or DIY project. (We aisle-surf all the time at HGTV!)

www.modernmasters.com
Check out Modern Masters for those hard-to-find faux finishing materials including metallic paints, glazes, and plasters. This is a great place to go while compiling your inspiration folder. You'll also find my favorite Skim Stone countertop product and materials here.

www.grahamandbrown.com
Go to Graham and Brown for the coolest wallpaper. You'll find patterns to fit an endless variety of styles and tones. The best part of Graham and Brown papers is the application process: You can actually put the glue directly on the wall, with no pasting and waiting! Then, if you ever want to remove it, it peels off easily and leaves a liner on the wall so you can reapply new paper or a paint.

www.greendepot.com

Shop Green Depot when starting a project and be amazed at what materials you can find a green substitute for. Prices are fair, and the selection of eco-friendly materials is wide and unique!

www.earthshade.com

Shop here for burlap window shades. Composed of an all-natural, heavyweight jute fabric laminated to fiberboard, these decorative, tackable shades are ideal for a range of applications from family rooms to children's bedrooms.

www.icestone.biz

IceStone is an ideal green countertop material made from 100 percent recycled glass mixed with cement. These gorgeous countertops are highly durable and beautiful and fit all design styles because they are totally customizable in color and finish.

www.ecosmartfire.com

Environmentally friendly open fireplaces, installable in walls, outdoors, or freestanding indoors. They are fueled by easily renewable denatured ethanol, which burns clean into steam, heat, and a miniscule amount of carbon dioxide. These fireplaces are virtually maintenance free.

www.lyptus.com

"Lyptus" is the trade name for ecologically responsibly harvested eucalyptus, which comes in a wide range of light and dark woods. Like bamboo, eucalyptus grows at a much quicker rate than other woods and is harvested from groves in Brazil and Australia dedicated to preventing deforestation.

www.consumerfed.org/energy/homeenergyefficiency.asp

The Consumer Federation of America has more information on how to find consultants who will walk you through all the prices and steps to improving home insulation.

www.eleekinc.com

Eleek is a lighting restoration service that speaks to the important concept of updating existing goods. Keep your beautiful old lamps and make them cheaper to turn on. When Eleek restores a light fixture, every piece of a fixture is taken apart, repaired, and restored to its original splendor.

www.energystar.gov

Energy Star provides information on home energy audits—snag those tax breaks! It's always a good idea to survey the latest ideas and recommendations from Energy Star when starting a new project.

www.natural-salt-lamps.com

Rock salt lamps add a natural style and harmony to your space—and a warm, ambient glow. These organic lights make for great conversation pieces in your home.

www.royaldesignstudio.com

Royal Design Studios offers an extensive selection of stencils, inspiring pictures, and how-tos that will help you put yours to use. Before starting your stencil project, check this site out for some cool tips.

www.prolightingsupplies.com

Gel filters to color your lighting can be found here; there is a wide selection and they're pretty affordable. It's an easy way to change the ambiance in a space.

www.ikea.com

No brainer! Buy cheap, stylish furnishings from IKEA and break out the DIY and faux-finishing skills you learned in this book to make them into something even more spectacular and totally your own!

www.ezfauxdecor.com

Specializes in a variety of faux-decor films for your home, such as stained glass, frosted glass, privacy window wallpaper, stainless steel, cork, and chalkboard. You just peel and stick it to any smooth surface and you can instantly change your décor.

www.steponart.com

Check out these canvas rug alternatives. You can even customize them by color and pattern—it's an affordable way to find a midpoint between carpet and floor. Place them on hard surfaces like wood, tile, concrete, or linoleum.

NOTABLE LOCATIONS

Chicago Merchandise Mart: www.mmart.com

Thanks to 2009 Chicago Dream Home Designers:

Laurel Feldman-Foyer
Living Room: Larry Boeder
Home Office: Janet McCann
Bathroom: Christopher Michiels
Bedroom: Missie Bender
Dining Room: Leslie Jones
Kitchen: Mick De Giulio
Library: Denise Antonucci, Jerry Sanfilippo
Veranda: Frank Fontana

Michaelian & Kohlberg: www.michaelian.com

Kenneth Ludwig Home: www.kennethludwig.com

Emerald Building: www.emeraldchicago.com

Special thanks for helping with locations:

Mary Jo Gordon Designs
222 Merchandise Mart Plaza
#1510 Chicago 60654
(312) 933 8948

DIY INDEX

Paper Bag Faux-Leather Wall Treatment 51

The Best Faux Finishes for Your Walls 52

Basket-weave Panels from Toilet Paper 55

Wallpapering With Fabric 56

Work Your Own Wainscot 56

Painting and Installing A Ceiling Medallion 62

Faux Beams 63

Bookshelf Conversion to Entry Storage 85

Picket Fence Storage Bench 86

The Multiple Frame Collage 87

Doorknob Coat Rack 88

The Standing Display Table 89

The Floating Catch-all Shelf 91

Cool Focal Wall Framing 100

Making Your Own Alternative to Area Rugs 102

Stylish, Energy-saving Radiator Cover 105

Pimp Your Pillows For Less 108

Mosaic End Table 108

Wooden Chair Makeover 109

Eclectic Storage Ottoman 110

Cigar Box Tabletop 112

Headboards and Illusions 118

Contemporary High Headboard 120

Custom Lampshade 124

Closet Mirror Conversion 125

Tiling the Wall Behind Your Stove 144

Adding More Dividers and Wine Glass
Storage to Cabinets 145

Recycled Window Pot Rack 146

Floor Clothes for your Kitchen or Pets 148

Picture Box Storage Cubicles 155

The Reclaimed Country-Style Desk 161

Customized Corkboard 162

Molding a Bookshelf 164

Magnetic Painted Wall with a Frame 166

The Sleek Modern Bar 175

The Tuck-Away Mobile Bar 177

Shadow Box Display Case 178

Wild Skateboard Picture Frame 180

The Candy Counter 182

Snazzy Sound Insulating 183

Classic Cinema Walls with
Black-And-White Posters 183

360-Degree Curtain Enclosure 184

ESSENTIAL TOOLS FOR DIY

Owning these things will make you ready to create new objects and change old ones:

* Safety goggles
* Paintbrushes (it's worth investing in a good set of brushes if you'll take care of them)
* Cordless drill (cordless means way less frustration)
* Staple gun (you'll be amazed at how many quick fixes can be accomplished with this)
* Hot glue gun (a necessity for any crafty type)
* Caulk gun
* Hammer
* Pliers
* Stud finder
* Level
* Clamps
* Handsaw
* Circle saw (or chop saw)

SPECIAL THANKS

There are so many great people in my life to thank, who made this book happen on so many levels . . . so if I forgot anyone, sorry. First off, I'd like to acknowledge my mom, dad, and sister for supporting and believing in me when I was just an ambitious wiseass with a dream. My girlfriend, Sherry, who was my rock, my support system, makeup artist, etc., and put up with months of late-night writing and sketching sessions, no Christmas decorations, an often messy house, paint, and other props that consumed our lives for months while we shot the photos for the book. To Steve Mandel and my literary agent, Joy Tutela at the David Black agency, who helped guide me through uncharted territory. To Dervla Kelly and the team at Stewart, Tabori & Chang, who believed enough in me to give me my first book deal. To "the prodigy" Luke Thomas, who with his writing brilliance took my words, style, and personality and helped shape this book into the fine work it is today. Thank you to the folks at Chicago Merchandise Mart, Kenneth Ludwig, and the Harrington Design school. Thank you to all my friends, and the homeowners who allowed me to shoot photos of their special places. Thank you to my girlfriend's dad, "Toots," who I depend upon to give me his brutally honest opinion and who extends his generosity whenever called upon. Thank you to my extended family at the *Today Show*, Kathie Lee, Hoda, Tammy Filler, and Sarah Clagett, who allow me to be a part of their crazy world month after month. A special thanks goes out to the folks at HGTV for giving me the opportunity to be a part of the legacy that is *Design on a Dime*.

Finally I would like to thank you, the readers, fans, and supporters who allow me to enter your homes through the magic of television and books. You gave this humble and grateful kid from New York a platform to share his creative vision. This is just the beginning—I hope we remain in each other's lives for a long time to come!

Sincerely,

FRANK FONTANA

Published in 2010 by Stewart, Tabori & Chang
An imprint of ABRAMS

Text copyright © 2010 Frank Fontana
Photographs copyright © 2010 Brian Willette
Additional photography provided by Gregory K. Porter Photography

Copeland Furniture, "Frank Lloyd Wright® Furniture by Copeland"
www.copelandfurniture.com

Library of Congress Cataloging-in-Publication Data

Fontana, Frank.
Frank Fontana's dirty little secrets of design / Frank Fontana.
p. cm.
Includes index.
ISBN 978-1-58479-855-2 (alk. paper)
1. Interior decoration—Amateurs' manuals. I. Title. II. Title: Dirty little secrets of design.
NK2115.F64 2010
747'.1—dc22
2010017140

Editor: Dervla Kelly
Cover design: Alissa Faden
Interior design: Laura Klynstra
Production Manager: Tina Cameron

The text of this book was composed in Fairfield & Lisboa.

Printed and bound in China
10 9 8 7 6 5 4 3 2 1

Stewart, Tabori & Chang books are available at special discounts when purchased in quantity for
premiums and promotions as well as fundraising or educational use. Special editions can also be created
to specification. For details, contact specialsales@abramsbooks.com or the address below.

THE ART OF BOOKS SINCE 1949
115 West 18th Street
New York, NY 10011
www.abramsbooks.com